Why delegate? Because your tim

THE POWER OF DELEGATION

SAVE TIME, SAVE MONEY AND GROW WITH VIRTUAL ASSISTANTS

Francesca Moi

Hello!

It's fantastic to see that you're interested to start delegating and reclaiming your time. If you're ready to hire a Virtual Assistant, I'd love to offer you a credit towards a free Virtual Assistant service, giving you the opportunity to experience firsthand the incredible impact of having someone work alongside you.

Simply scan the code below to get started!

Looking forward to hearing from you.

GIFT
VOUCHER

Free Virtual Assistant

This exclusive Gift Voucher entitles you to a $500 credit towards hiring your next Virtual Assistant.

TO:

EXPIRY DATE:

To claim please scan the QR code to book a call with our team.

Terms and condition: This voucher is not redeemable for cash and can only be used for Empowering Virtual Solutions-related services. This voucher is non-transferable and must be redeemed by booking your service prior to the expiration date.
The virtual assistant service is subject to availability and must be scheduled in advance.

First published by Ultimate World Publishing 2024
Copyright © 2024 Francesca Moi

ISBN

Paperback - 978-1-923255-61-6
Ebook - 978-1-923255-62-3

Cover design: Ultimate World Publishing
Layout and typesetting: Ultimate World Publishing
Editor: Vanessa McKay

Ultimate World Publishing
Diamond Creek,
Victoria Australia 3089
www.writeabook.com.au

ULTIMATE WORLD
—— PUBLISHING ——

TESTIMONIALS

∞

As a long-time client of Francesca, I've had the privilege of working with two of her exceptional Virtual Assistants, and I'm currently in the process of adding a third for our Marketing Department. 'The Power of Delegation' has been a game-changer for me. This book perfectly encapsulates the essence of efficiently scaling a business while regaining time to focus on CEO big picture strategies of business growth. Francesca's strategies, especially on leveraging VAs, have significantly enhanced my operational efficiency. Her insights are practical and transformative, offering a clear path to success by delegating effectively. I highly recommend this book to any business owner looking to grow their business and improve their quality of life

Nando Barnett - Sell in Style
https://sellinstyle.com.au/

There is gold in this book! It's not just about outsourcing tasks; it's about reclaiming your time, focusing on what matters, and transforming how you run your business. Whether you're overwhelmed with daily chores or struggling to grow, these insights into building a reliable virtual team will empower you to work smarter, not harder. A must-read for anyone serious about taking their business to the next level!

Wendy Goni Mendez - XDesigns Advertising
https://xdesigns.com.au/

I have gotten to know Francesca through several business networks. I have also had the privilege of learning about her journey through her events as well as on a personal level. It didn't take me long to realise how switched on Francesca is as a businesswoman and how passionate she is about living a meaningful life and teaching others to do the same.

Having gone through the ups and downs associated with running several businesses, Francesca learnt a great deal about business and herself, knowledge she can now pass on to others. With Empowering Virtual Solution, she truly aligned her work with a life she loves living and teaches her clients to do the same. She really is the queen of delegating.

From educating others on the mental blocks behind delegating to teaching them the step-by-step process of hiring and onboarding their VAs, to mindfully crafting tasks and managing time effectively, this book will give you lots of great tips on outsourcing and doing it wisely. Delegating in a way that will save you time and not add to your already full plate, which truly is key in my view.

Having gone through the process of hiring my own VA through Francesca, I found this book invaluable in understanding in detail how to make my journey with the EVS team more efficient and enjoyable.

If you are struggling to manage your time, getting overwhelmed with various tasks or their volume, or getting behind on your emails or other key priorities in the business (like I was before I hired my VA), this book is for you!

So strap in and enjoy the journey! It really is worth it.

Polina Rodchenko - Polina Rodchenko Interiors
https://www.polinaradchenko.com/

'The Power of Delegation' is a must-read for every business owner looking to take control of their time and scale their operations. Francesca breaks down the art of delegation and shows how Virtual Assistants can revolutionise a business by allowing the owner to focus on their core strengths.

The practical strategies she shares are not just theory but real life-tested insights that will save time, cut unnecessary costs, and drive real growth. Her engaging writing style makes the complex process of building and managing a remote team feel accessible, even for beginners. This book is a game-changer for anyone ready to work smarter, not harder. I highly recommend it to anyone serious about achieving both personal and professional success through the power of delegation!

Natasa Denman - Ultimate 48 Hour Author
https://www.writeabook.com.au/

Wow! Francesca's latest book is a game changer! I only wish I had this knowledge sooner! If you're looking to maximise your time, increase wealth, and bring more prosperity into your life, mastering the art of working with virtual assistants is absolutely essential. This book is a must-read, offering incredible insights on leading effectively and being supported by smart, streamlined processes. A true blueprint for success!"

William Farmer - Dale Carnegie Australia
https://www.dalecarnegie.com/

Francesca Moi's The Power of Delegation is a game-changer for business owners who want to streamline their operations and maximise the efficiency of their virtual assistants. As an online marketing strategist who works with business owners and their VAs to improve marketing management, I found her approach both insightful and practical. Francesca expertly covers the essentials of delegation, showing how to save time, reduce stress, and boost productivity while driving business growth. Her clear guidance on managing teams, effective onboarding, and scaling with a VA aligns perfectly with the strategies I use in my work. Francesca's expertise, combined with her actionable advice, makes this book an indispensable resource for any business owner serious about achieving sustainable growth through smart team management.

Chantal Gerardy - Online Business Marketing
www.chantalgerardy.com.au

"The Power of Delegation: Save Time, Save Money and Grow with Virtual Assistants"

Francesca! Five stars to you and congratulations. It was a privilege to read and provide this testimonial on such a wonderful book.

"The Power of Delegation" by Francesca Moi is an absolute game-changer for any entrepreneur or business leader looking to scale efficiently. This book brilliantly outlines how leveraging Virtual Assistants can revolutionise your business by freeing up time, reducing costs, and allowing you to focus on growth and strategy. With Francesca's practical insights and actionable steps, it demystifies the delegation process, showing how to build a capable team of Virtual Assistants who can work diligently with their clients to handle everything from routine tasks to complex projects. Whether you're just starting out or are an experienced leader, this book is an indispensable guide for optimising productivity and unlocking the true potential of your business.

Catherine Halse - Chameleon Confidential Solutions
https://www.chameleonconfidentialsolutions.com/

Francesca Moi is the queen of delegation! Not only is she a leader on the subject, but I witness her walk the talk in her own business. In her 4th book, *"THE POWER OF DELEGATION: Save Time, Save Money and Grow with Virtual Assistants"*, Francesca shares the practical secrets that have enabled her to grow multiple 7-figure businesses through the power of delegation. A must-read for every business owner.

Russell Pearson - FORGE Business Program
https://russellpearson.com/

ACKNOWLEDGEMENTS

∞

My fourth book… Who would have thought? A huge thank you to Natasa Denman, who inspired me and pushed me to become an author for the first time back in 2015. She was the one who suggested I write *Follow Me – Shutttup and Build Your Network*, followed by *Bums on Seats*, then *Invisible to Invincible*, and now this latest work.

English is not my first language, and reaching this milestone feels absolutely huge.

A heartfelt thank you to my amazing team of Virtual Assistants who have supported me for over 10 years now. Bebs, Dee, Maria, Joann, Vine, Rei and Jhomz – you are the backbone of this journey. Thank you, thank you, thank you!

To Lina, my right-hand woman in business, thank you for bringing all my ideas to life and for meticulously reviewing this book before it went to print.

To my mom, Adriana, for being my biggest fan and always having my back; to my dad, Antonello, for his unwavering belief in me and for believing in me and the success of this business.

And a huge thank you to all my clients and followers. None of this would have been possible without you!

CONTENTS

PREFACE

∞

The Concept of Delegation...

Delegation often seems like a distant dream. We think, *if only I could delegate this task to someone else!* But turning that wish into reality is easier said than done.

When you first see someone messaging and delegating daily tasks, you may wonder *isn't it faster to just do it?* How do you explain to someone that it isn't?

It happens a lot to me when I'm out and about, and people ask me, *"Do you want to catch up on this day, at this time?"*

And I say, *"Yes, sure. Let me check out my calendar."*
Then, I check my calendar and if I see a spot that is available, I will message my VA and say, *"Hey, Bebsie, can you please make sure that you put this in the calendar and invite this person and we're going to meet them at this place?"* while that person is right next to me.

They're like, *"Wait a minute! You're sending the message to your VA in the Philippines to tell her to put it in your calendar? But can't you do it here, now?"*

1

I'm like, *"Why?"*

Then they'll say, *"Isn't it faster if you just do it? It'll take a second."*

We have standards, and we have concepts and procedures we want to stick to in our business. I'm the CEO, I don't have time to really go in and put it in the calendar - I mean, I could have time, don't get me wrong, I could do it, but when I do it, there's more likely to be mistakes because I'm not a very detailed person and it's not my area of expertise - putting something in the calendar. I'd probably miss some details, and probably be wondering on the day *where are we meeting again?* Because there's nothing on the calendar. So I'd rather let my VA do what she does best and not interfere and create confusion.

My VA structures my calendar, she colour-codes it, so it's easy for me to look at it and know when I have a meeting, how to prepare for it and when I need to get ready.

These are different concepts, different procedures that we have in place. This is why we delegate, because we should not be the ones focusing on details. Our VA should. We should not look after things that are not at our level of expertise. We should let our Virtual Assistants do what they do best. As a CEO, I should be able to focus here with the person I'm talking to and enjoy the conversation. Choose a time, send it to my VA, and she'll work it out. If you need to reschedule, the details are with my VA because she's the one who organised the meeting. It will take the pressure off me. It will take so much off my plate.

Your Time is Valuable...

I have become a master of delegation because I chose to. I realised that time is money. I chose to truly believe that delegation was going to give me a lot of money back, and it has, and I will continue doing it.

Note to self: Delegate to the Right People. *Instead of asking, "How can I do this?" focus on "Who can do this for me?" to achieve goals more efficiently.*

I delegate everything. I literally delegate from my cleaning, my laundry, my cooking, washing of my car, my garden, grocery shopping - everything. If I can delegate something, I will. Because my time is valuable, and I don't want to spend it doing chores. I don't want to spend time doing things that are not helping me to reach my goals. I've got specific goals in my business, specific goals in my life. I want to have a beautiful, loving family. If I'm spending the weekend cleaning, I'm going to be a grumpy family member. A grumpy wife. A grumpy mother. A grumpy daughter. Grumpy at everything, and I don't want to be that.

I choose delegation to meet the best version of myself. And this is exactly why I'm writing this book. I want to show everybody why delegation is a must. Without delegation, I couldn't scale my business. Without delegation, I would be completely stuck where I was back in the beginning. I couldn't do everything. I had to stop trying and start delegating because I couldn't just keep reacting to the business and keep doing it all myself. I couldn't keep juggling all those responsibilities. I had to let go of something and give it to someone else while trusting that they were going to do a better job than me, because I was trying to do too much. I couldn't focus on growing the business if I were stuck in it. So, I had to let go of all the little things that were stopping me from getting my business to the next level.

I had to understand all that because it's one of the vital steps and one of our vital problems that I'm going to talk about in this book. How much we business owners get attached to the fact that we can do it all. And we can. We did it at the beginning, and it was well done. Congratulations! You have gotten the business this far. It's amazing. Whatever you've done until now will not get the business to where you want to take it. To soar to the next version of ourselves and our desired CEO status, we need to let go of many things.

Note to self: Delegate for freedom. Delegating gives you freedom from tasks that drain energy.

The Importance of Leveraging Time Through Others...

There are so many benefits in hiring someone to do the work for you. You can hire someone in Australia or any other country you're located. It's possible and it's very simple, correct? You hire someone and pay task-based or project-based, and they'll do the things that you need them to do.

But a lot of small business owners cannot afford someone right away in our country; it's quite expensive. So we need to find a way to really leverage the world and be able to actually give an opportunity to someone that might not have such a beautiful opportunity in their lives to work from their own home and really make a difference in your life, as we can make a difference in theirs. It's a win-win situation.

4

Note to self: Focus on Strengths. Concentrate on your strengths while others handle the rest.

The Benefits...

The benefit for us, as business owners, is that not only are we making a difference in someone's life, but we're also resting - we are restoring our energy so that we can actually be more productive with our time. We will finally be able to return to having holidays and spending time with our families, which is vital. Remember when we wanted to start the business in the first place? We had countless ideas, dreams, and options, but once we started a business, we worked nonstop.

That is not why we started a business, right?

We started a business to spend time with our family. So let's do it, let's actually do it. We're going to work smarter, not harder. And we're going to have more time to work on the business to take it to a whole new level.

Three main benefits of hiring a VA:

1. Save TIME
2. Save MONEY
3. Save YOU

Once you hire a VA you will see after 2-3 months that you have saved time, money and yourself from burnout. And your business would have made a lot of money from this priceless decision to invest in a VA.

The Queen of Delegation...

I am very passionate about this, and I became the queen of delegation. Everybody talks to me about, *"How do you delegate so much? What do you do? How do you not stay a control freak?"*

I'm a recovering control freak. I wanted to micromanage my team. I wanted to do it all. But eventually, I realised that my own perfectionism, my own control freakiness, was stopping the business from going to the next level.

I had to learn. I had no choice but to learn - learn to let it go to go to the next level.

Note to self: Delegate, Don't Abdicate. *Stay engaged, but don't micromanage the work you delegate.*

Who is this book for?

This book is tailored for anyone who values their time and seeks to optimise it. Whether you're a business owner, a solopreneur, or a manager. It's designed to resonate with a wide range of professionals, from those just embarking on their entrepreneurial journey to established business leaders aiming to refine their operations and focus on growth.

If you are a **new entrepreneur,** this book will guide you through the essential steps of leveraging your time effectively from the start. You'll learn how to avoid common pitfalls that consume valuable hours and how to set a strong foundation for efficient practices.

For the **established business owner,** the strategies discussed will help you reassess and recalibrate your current operations. It's about refining advanced techniques to save time, enhance productivity, and scale your business to new heights.

Managers and **team leaders** will find valuable insights into delegating effectively, enhancing team productivity, and fostering an environment where time management is a shared priority.

Ultimately, if you believe that time is money and seek to maximise both, this book will show you practical ways to streamline your processes, delegate non-core tasks, and focus on what truly matters. By the end of this book, you'll not only have a clearer understanding of how to save time but also how to transform that time into a more fulfilling and impactful professional and personal life.

Reason for Writing This Book

One of my clients shared her struggles with me, which really struck a chord. She runs her business and finds herself buried under a mountain of tasks. From managing teams to making sure orders on their new online sales portal go smoothly, she's handling it all.

She's deep into everything – from marketing to managing finances, a role her husband is also trying to step away from. She's wearing so many hats and, honestly, it's overwhelming.

She told me, *"I'm doing it all, and it's just too much."*

This book was inspired by her story and many others like her. It's for all business owners out there who are tired of managing every single thing by themselves and feeling stretched too thin. I want to show you how to lighten your load by delegating tasks effectively and organising your work better.

We're going to explore ways to free up your time so you can focus more on growing your business and taking some well-deserved time for yourself.

The Common Mistakes when Delegating...

I want you to avoid this one now – stop thinking, *'It's just faster if I do it.'*

If I do it, I know that it's done properly. But if I do it, I also know it's going to take an entire week, and an entire week of my time is a lot of money for the business. I realised it wouldn't be faster if I just did it. It was slower, and it was way more expensive. When I explain to my VA how to do things properly, it is faster and more cost effective if they do it.

Once I allowed my team to become experts in their own tasks, they became faster and better. So, if I now compare myself, my skills in *Canva*, and my team's skills in *Canva*, I can't even compare. I am like a dinosaur. I don't even know what to click on. My team can pull up a poster in three seconds.

In the beginning, I was showing my first VA how to use *Canva*. I was not that good, but I was still faster and better because I was doing it more often than her. Eventually, my VA surpassed me and they can now do it better. And this is when I realised it wasn't faster if I just did it, I was simply a little bit more experienced because I was doing it for a little bit longer but as soon as I gave the opportunity to someone to do it for me, then they became so much faster, and so much better than me. And it was so much easier for both of us and the business.

It wasn't about me micromanaging them and doing it with them, saying, *"Do this or that,"* and then staying on top of their breath and not letting them actually explore the task – it was more about supporting them, letting go, trusting, and allowing them to play and make mistakes because we all learn from mistakes.

What to expect...

In this book, you're going to learn about how to delegate and what to delegate and how to hire someone who is an A Player, how to recognise A Players in your business, and how to onboard them so that you actually help them succeed inside your business.

This book will help you transform your approach to work and time management because we'll show you exactly how to leverage your time, how to make the most of your day so that you can also help your Virtual Assistant make the most of their days, and how to have a super productive meeting with your Virtual Assistant.

Here's the deal: There's only one way to fix your overworking problem: confront it directly. You can't ignore it any longer. In the next chapters, we'll guide you through the steps to take action. It's time to draw a line in the sand and embrace accountability.

Take action now: Email me at *info@empoweringvirtualsolution.com* with the subject line: *"I am ready to work less and delegate more."* Tell me you're committed to doing whatever it takes to reclaim your time and live the life you deserve, working no more than 20 hours a week. If you're all in, let me know. Send that email, make that commitment – I want to hear from you!

Every week, during our team huddle, my VA will present a report of your emails, ensuring I'm updated on all your messages, and you'll receive a response from us.

I'm excited to hear from you soon!

CHAPTER 1

UNDERSTANDING YOUR VIRTUAL ASSISTANT

∞

Virtual Assistants are real people. When we are referring to VA, we don't mean AI. This is not Artificial Intelligence, these are actual humans. In our agency, we hire Virtual Assistants from the Philippines.

Virtual Assistants can take on administrative roles in your business and serve as an EA (Executive Assistant) for you. With the correct training, they can handle anything.

Thanks to the help of a remote team, I was able to grow two different businesses to seven figures. Working with a local team differs completely from working with a remote team. The thing that I like the most is the freedom I get. I am not obligated to stay in the office. I can work from anywhere, even from the side of my pool. Hiring remotely has provided me with the freedom I value.

In my first business, I was sceptical of the skills of the VAs, so I would hire locally assuming that VAs could not be as good as someone local. But to be honest, they had the skills, but I didn't. I didn't know how to delegate to someone that wasn't physically next to me. I didn't know how to make the most of a VA. I assumed they would never be reliable and able to do things without my presence, so I didn't spend time training them.

It took me years, but eventually I learned.

To delegate parts of the business to my remote team, I had to dedicate as much time to them as I did to training the local team. I introduced co-working… Some days I spent most of my day on *Zoom* with my VAs working together like I would do with a local team member. Just co-working in silence, so they could ask me questions. I only do this when we are working on a project or when I am teaching them a new task. It was a game-changer.

The biggest challenge I had at the beginning was not being able to read social cues, I didn't know how to be of support to my VA. If a local team member was having a bad day I could tell, from their face, from their energy and from the way they would interact in the office, but with the online remote team I had no chance to see those things. I had to learn.

I had to implement meetings and huddles to motivate them. Working from home can be great, but since COVID, we all know it can also be challenging and disconnecting. It is our responsibility, as CEOs, to bridge that gap.

I also had to coach my local team on interacting with the VAs, reminding them to fully integrate them into the team. This included doing quick huddles on *Slack*, using emojis in comments, and being extra considerate and not too blunt, since written comments can easily be misinterpreted. Taking a few extra seconds to be mindful of how a comment or feedback we give is crucial.

I cannot imagine running a business without a remote team to be there to support us and save us time, energy and money.

The benefit of hiring Virtual Assistants remotely is that they are a lot more cost effective than what we can hire locally, or wherever you are in the world. And it is important to understand that because we hire Virtual Assistants remotely, we can really bring more economy into our own country.

Some may question why I haven't focused on hiring locally, but our remote hiring strategy has significantly contributed to our business growth, enabling us to eventually afford local hires as well. We have found that many professionals in developing countries have a strong sense of gratitude and dedication to their roles, appreciating both the opportunity and the flexibility that remote work provides.

I value the extra loyalty, commitment and responsibility my VAs provide. They're very responsible and very excited and passionate about the role. I love that! Who doesn't? We can change lives and make it possible for a Virtual Assistant to visit Australia once a year. Working in a company like ours provides opportunities they might never have otherwise.

A common misconception about hiring a Virtual Assistant (VA) is the belief that they may lack proficiency in English. However, in the Philippines, English is widely spoken and is an official language, much like Italian is to me as someone who was born in Italy. In fact, studies show that 55% of adult Filipinos speak English, and the Philippines ranks 20th among 113 countries for English proficiency.* This places Filipino VAs on par with many native English speakers in terms of communication skills. While it's true that you might need to double-check certain tasks, doing so is often much quicker than handling everything from scratch.

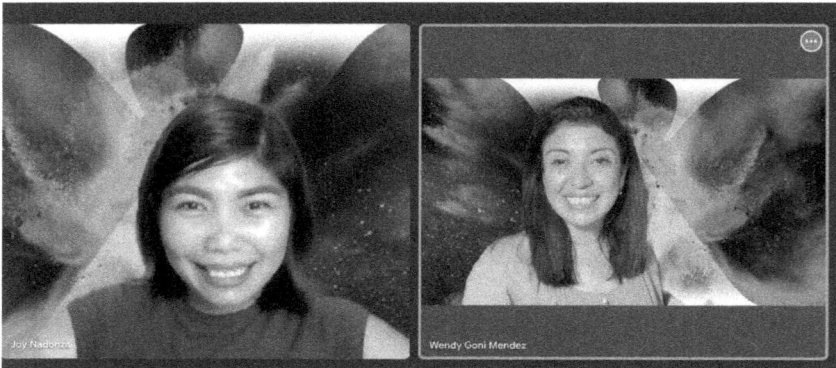

I always remember to bear this in mind. People think they don't understand properly. I am Italian and I was one of those people too!

* (Reference: *https://www.ef.com/wwen/epi/*)

And that's also incorrect. If we are clear about our expectations, if we're clear on our task delegation, if we don't mumble, we don't hop on our words, the Virtual Assistant can understand us well. It's amusing to me when Virtual Assistants struggle to comprehend my accent.

Communication, especially when working across languages, requires patience from both parties. One thing I realise is that patience is essential when interacting with someone who is speaking a second language. Some native English speakers may not fully appreciate the challenges of learning and using a second language, simply because they haven't experienced it themselves. Understanding this can foster more effective and compassionate communication.

So, having a bit of compassion for someone who had the courage to learn a second language from scratch and speak it fluently and write and work with that second language is quite admirable. Besides, there is technology nowadays, something like Grammarly or AIs, that they can use to check their grammar.

Unfortunately, in some cultures, particularly in the Philippines, VAs are often very deferential, commonly responding with, *"Yes, Ma'am"* or *"Yes, Sir!"* This has sometimes led to them not speaking up when they're struggling, reaching a breaking point where they just burnout and vanish. This disappearance often leaves employers puzzled and worried, wondering what happened. To address this, we've been actively training our Virtual Assistants to speak up. If they're struggling, they should speak up. If they feel bullied, they should speak up. It's crucial that they understand they shouldn't just accept these situations for fear of losing their jobs. One of our core values is *"We always got your back."* This emphasises our commitment to supporting them, ensuring they feel valued within our community and in their roles. We've had VAs who thankfully reached out to us, expressing concerns like, *"My boss is rude to me,"* or *"My boss dumps tasks on me without clear instructions, leaving me lost."* When this happens, we take it seriously. We listen and review any available recordings or evidence. Then, we reach out to the client directly. It's important to remember that there's a human being on the other side. Having been in stressful business situations myself, I understand the pressure. Sometimes I wasn't the best boss, and I needed someone to tell me when I wasn't being fair. Acknowledging this helps me manage the emotional roller coaster of business. I try to foster an environment where it's okay to say, *"I'm stressed today. Please help me understand what's going wrong."* By being open and honest, rather than upset and disrespectful, builds a supportive team dynamic. In the past, I had to learn how to better manage my emotions, and together with Lina, we train business owners to create an environment that VAs love, ensuring they genuinely enjoy their work.

When I hire a Virtual Assistant, I have a five-minute talk with them to say, *"Look, I am different from other people; you're never going to be in trouble with me unless you lie, unless you don't tell me the truth, unless you avoid telling me the truth. As long as you have a problem, and you let me know immediately, as soon as you know, and we fix it together, you're never going to be in trouble. I'm always going to be here for you."*

And that gives them a little bit of confidence. And then, obviously, I need to follow up on that. So, if they make a mistake, I'll be like, *"Don't worry; I've got your back."* We are then good to go, and we solve things together!

To help us make that matching process very successful, we get our clients and our Virtual Assistant to do a test. We use the 16

Personality Tests. With the 16 personalities, we will see the strengths of a Virtual Assistant and a client and whether they match or not. This has been successful for us ever since. In our Agency we proudly have a 92% successful rate on the first match. We spend over five weeks to get to know our VAs in training so that when we match we know their strengths and match them accordingly.

The evolution of Virtual Assistants from administrative tasks to specialised services has gone so far that sometimes we no longer see the difference between recurring tasks and casual tasks. We have clients that struggle with giving a Virtual Assistant some tasks, and every day, they're stressed and are like, *"Oh my gosh! What am I going to give to my VA today?"*

And I'm like, *"Wait a minute, why are you trying to build a daily task? That's more work for you. Why don't you create some recurring tasks with the VA?"*

That is one of the biggest challenges a lot of business owners have today. They don't realise that the more recurring tasks we create for our Virtual Assistants, the more freedom they have. The more independent the VA will be, the more responsible they will become because the more we give them tasks every day, the more we micromanage them and we're not letting them own their role. I make it clear for my team to define their role in the company and what their role entails. What are the KPIs? What are the expectations? What do they need to create with a role? What do they need to do every day? So, If I'm not there, I'm not going to be, *"What are you working on today? What are you doing today? If I haven't given you any tasks, can you do anything?"*

For me, it's the opposite. I know my team has plenty of work to do. They know what I'm expecting out of all the projects or the things that I have in the business. And I don't need to micromanage, I can just show up in the meetings and see the results and see what they've done and maybe direct them a little better. That is all I need to do.

By consistently performing specialised tasks, such as administrative duties that need to be completed regularly, we can significantly reduce overtime and increase efficiency in our workflow. Staying on top of emails each week by organising and filing them away not only makes it easier to manage but also prevents the feeling of overwhelm that can arise from an overloaded inbox. When there are 2,000 unread emails sitting in the inbox, it becomes very easy to miss important messages, making it quite challenging to organise them effectively and respond promptly. Consistent action in managing these tasks builds momentum and creates a sense of freedom for everyone involved, leading to improved productivity and a more streamlined work environment. By prioritising these habits, we enable ourselves and our teams to work more efficiently, stay organised, and focus on what truly matters in our business.

When we mention specialised services, we are specifically talking about project-based work. At the moment, we're writing a book. My Virtual Assistants and I are working on this project together. I'm recording and the VA is transcribing, and then we're going to edit it together, create the cover, and do all the tasks together. This is a project where I've got a role. I need to unpack the book and speak it, and the VA needs to transcribe and edit it. We work together and are clear about each other's role.

To avoid giving tasks daily at the expense of our precious time, we need to create recurring tasks to do daily, weekly and monthly to avoid bottlenecks and forgetting things because that's what happens when we keep giving random ad hoc tasks. It will just set up the VA for failure.

My Virtual Assistants are running the business right now; they've been with me for over seven years. We built such a strong relationship that often, I'm the one asking questions to my VA instead of the other way around. I've hired a Virtual Assistant with no experience, and I prefer to hire based on attitude because that gives me the Virtual Assistant's loyalty. They are very loyal to me. They're very keen and very excited to work with us.

In our agency, we also train virtual assistants in organic marketing strategies for our clients. In my business, I've been teaching organic marketing strategies to business owners for over ten years. We've been showing them how to leverage building a personal brand and how to use reels, *Instagram, LinkedIn,* and *Facebook* to maximise that momentum and add value to the world. So hopefully, that will build trust with the people that I mentioned who want to work with us. Thus, we have trained VAs to be real social media managers who post or schedule content on different social media platforms, create graphics, create videos, and so on.

Our clients keep their VAs for extended periods because of the valuable contributions they provide, which is why our retainer is strong. We provide training for the VA. We are training them in AI now because it's the next big thing.

And speaking of that, I want to show you some case studies of successful Virtual Assistant partnerships. Here are three case studies that show how our clients are leveraging the use of Virtual Assistants.

*Note to self: **Abundance Mentality**. There are plenty of talented people who can help you achieve your goals.*

Case Study 1:
Meet Lainie, founder of *One Family Yoga, Pilates & Fitness* in Holland Park. For 11 years, she built a vibrant community with over 75 weekly classes. Overwhelmed by admin tasks, she hired VA Mary through Empowering Virtual Solution, transforming her business and allowing her to focus on teaching and engaging with her community.

Industry: Health and Wellness
Business: *One Family Yoga & Fitness*
Length with us: 14 Months
Activities done by VA: 80% social media management, 20% admin
Title of the role if hired in Australia: Social media coordinator
What this client would pay for this role in Australia: $70K Annual
Total investment VA: $28K Annual
Net saving per year: $42K

Case Study 2:
Introducing Lauren, a dedicated teacher who transitioned into a life and leadership coach at Taylor Made Change. With three years of business experience, Lauren specialises in corporate team coaching. The addition of her Virtual Assistant, Kath, revolutionised her social media strategy, allowing her to cultivate a robust online community on *Instagram*, *Facebook*, and *LinkedIn*. Their collaboration has led to substantial growth in both revenue and engagement.

Industry: Health and Wellness (Coaching)
Business: *Taylor Made Change*
Length with us: 28 Months
Activities done by VA: 80% social media management, 20% admin
Title of the role if hired in Australia: Social media coordinator
What this client would pay for this role in Australia: $70K Annual
Total investment VA: $28K Annual
Net saving per year: $42K

Case Study 3:
Meet Paul, a seasoned business owner from Melbourne managing a thriving company with $3.5 million in turnover. His team consists of 13 employees spread between the warehouse and the office, including a part-time sales manager.

Industry: Distribution
Business: *PMD Distributors*
Role Details: EA
What this client would pay for this role in Australia: $80K
Total investment VA: $32K Annual
Net saving per year: $48K

Paul's Experience:
"I manage a solid team in Melbourne, but it's challenging as we try to grow. I'm swamped daily with non-essential emails, taking up precious time. I realised I'm now the bottleneck of my bussiness as I have a long list of things to approve and I don't have time to get to it." Paul explained.

He added, *"Your podcast 'Business Behind the Scenes', inspired me to delegate more effectively and avoid CEO pitfalls. I see the need to start with a VA for emails and then possibly expand to handle more complex tasks."*

Paul is eager to start: *"I'm ready to talk about strategic delegation, beginning with one VA and expanding as necessary to balance efficiency and growth."*

He concluded optimistically, *"I'm looking forward to partnering with you to streamline our operations and propel PMD Distributors forward."*

Case Study 4:
Meet Nando and Sarah, a dynamic husband-and-wife team, took over Sell in Style Property Styling in early 2020. Leveraging their seven years of experience in property development, interior decorating, and project management, they transformed it into one of Brisbane's top home staging companies. With an annual revenue of $2.5 million and a reputation for creating high-impact interiors, Nando and Sarah are setting new benchmarks in the home staging industry across Australia.

Industry: Property Styling
Business: *Sell in Style Property Styling*
Team Composition: 32 Office Team Members, 2 Virtual Assistants
Role Details: EA + VA (Admin Assistant)

What this client would pay for this role in Australia:
$80K +$50K = $130K
Total investment VA: $64K
Net saving per year: $66K

Challenges and Solutions: As the business grew, the assistant manager was swamped with 300-400 daily inquiries, prompting Nando and his partner Sarah to hire a Virtual Assistant (VA) through Empowering Virtual Solutions. This addition significantly improved efficiency.

Impact of Hiring a VA: *"The VA drastically reduced our workload and increased our efficiency,"* Nando stated. Encouraged by industry mentors, he also hired an Executive Assistant (EA) to manage daily tasks, allowing him to focus on strategy. "The EA has transformed our operations, making them smoother and more effective with tools like Loom for clear communication," he noted.

"Adding a VA has been a game-changer, reducing stress and enhancing our productivity. This partnership has propelled our business forward, and I'm excited about our future prospects," Nando reflected on the positive changes brought by integrating virtual assistance into their workflow.

Key Takeaways:

- VAs can handle both front and back-end tasks, becoming more skilled over time.
- Understand cultural differences; VAs from the Philippines are loyal and hardworking but may avoid confrontation. Training them to communicate openly is crucial.

- Emphasise honesty and clear communication to build strong, trusting relationships with VAs.
- Assign recurring tasks to VAs to reduce micromanagement and empower them to take ownership of their roles.
- VAs can handle complex, project-based tasks, contributing to long-term business success.
- Hiring based on attitude fosters loyalty. Ongoing training, especially in new skills like AI, keeps VAs valuable.
- Hiring remote VAs is cost-effective and supports global economic opportunities.
- Address misconceptions about language skills; patience and clear communication are key when working with VAs from non-English speaking backgrounds.
- Fact: Most Filipino VAs are very good English Speakers!
- Spending time with VAs training them to your business expectation is the shortcut everyone is looking for.
- Case studies are great social proof why VAs are the game-changer your business needs.

What actions are you going to take from this chapter?

1 _____

_____

_____

_____

_____

2 _____

_____

_____

_____

_____

3 _____

_____

_____

_____

_____

CHAPTER 2

THE ART OF
DELEGATION

∞

In this chapter, what I would love to share with you is understanding how delegation works, what it is, and what it is not. The psychological barriers to delegation and how to overcome them, as well as common misconceptions to effective delegation. Understanding what is the expectation that we have around delegation and how to do it, identifying tasks to delegate, and distinguishing between high-value tasks and time-consuming tasks that can be delegated.

By the end of this chapter, you will understand what exactly you should delegate to a Virtual Assistant and how to delegate those tasks because delegation is a skill that we need to all really chip in and learn.

This chapter can be for you, the CEO or for your team. We find a lot of our clients' local team members struggle to delegate to a VA.

They often feel threatened and think it's better and faster if they do it, so as you read this, think about your team - are they delegating? Are they wasting time and money? Are there any tasks that they could delegate so they could focus on money making activities?

If you or your team ignore delegation, nothing will ever change. You will be overwhelmed, tired, and exhausted forever. We really need to understand that, in delegation, there will never be the right time to delegate. This is what people tell me most of the time,

"I'm not ready to delegate." And I ask, *"When are you going to be ready?"*

You're never going to be ready because if we keep ignoring that we need to delegate, and if we keep moving forward *because I'm very busy now, I should do it later on*; that day will never come because you're always going to be busy until you delegate. And so we need to really acknowledge that there's never going to be a right time to delegate. The right time to delegate is today or maybe yesterday!!

I'm sure that you don't want to be overwhelmed. I'm sure that you don't want to continue to be stressed. I'm sure that you don't want to work 24/7. And if that's you, if you're ready to have your time back, your life back, then keep reading, because this is exactly what this chapter will teach you.

Note to self: Letting Go of Control. Trusting others and relinquishing control is crucial for maximising efficiency. Micromanaging limits creativity and progress.

Delegation is not micromanaging people. We need to watch our limiting beliefs about what we do and how we do it. A lot of us think, *Oh, it's just faster if I do it.* If you have a belief that it is going to be faster if you do it, then when you delegate, you're going to be someone that tries to micromanage people. You must be someone who will try to do it with the VA or do it for the VA. What I mean is that there is a step in the delegation process that you do with your VA, and that's vital. But then, eventually, let go. Let them make mistakes and you have to let them do their thing so that you can actually step into working ON the business and not IN the business. If you keep micromanaging your Virtual Assistant, nothing will get off your shoulders. You will be busier because you are working with the VA doing their tasks and you're working on your business as well. So, you will not have your time back. You're going to have more stress. You will drown even deeper.

And this is where a lot of people tell me, *"Francesca, it's not worth having a Virtual Assistant. I've done it in the past. I was so much busier and then I thought, it is faster if I just do it."*

This is the micromanaging type of people. The people who are control freaks, and they cannot really let go. How do I know? Because I was this person myself! I didn't want to learn how to delegate. I didn't want to step into the next level of being a CEO. I wanted to keep things as they were.

A lot of people complain about being busy. They just truly don't want to change because change is difficult, and change is hard. Learning how to delegate is not easy. But if we don't do it, then the consequences are even bigger. It is even harder to continue living like that rather than having a little bit of discomfort for the first couple of months to learn, *"Okay, these are the things that I need to delegate and the things that I need to let go of."*

Note to self: Avoid Task Hoarding. *Don't fall into the trap of hoarding tasks out of fear of failure.*

Delegating is not about meeting 24/7 with your Virtual Assistant because your Virtual Assistant will not be productive if you keep them on *Zoom* all day. You also will not be productive. Nobody can get their work done. But it's also important that we have some things that we need to do together. For example, I am recording this audio for this book. I am doing it with my Virtual Assistant. Why?

First, most of it is accountability, and it helps my Virtual Assistant and I to multitask while I'm recording. They can do other things in the background - but they can also listen and see if I'm saying something wrong. They can direct me on the things that I'm going to say. They can see how else they can use this recording for and not have to sit there and watch it back because they are already listening to it live. They're hearing my book while I'm here speaking it out loud. So that is the benefit of having a Virtual Assistant here - accountability and companionship is priceless to me!

There will be some things that you want to do with your Virtual Assistant, and there will be some things that you have to let go of and let your Virtual Assistant do. And then you can just check them until you know your VA is reliable, and they can do things without your supervision.

The Virtual Assistants cannot do some things that you delegate unless you teach them how to do it. Delegation is not like, *hey, this needs to be done, boom, do it*. If you want a task done, what I always recommend is to jump in a meeting, brainstorm what needs to be done, and brainstorm the phases of that project:

- Phase one, we need to make sure that the team takes all the information from my brain.
- Phase two is that the VA puts all the information into a platform.
- Phase three is that we meet and check.
- Phase four is the VA to implement it all.

This is an example of what could be a task delegated to someone. We need to either teach the VA how to do something or we need to help them structure the project to set them up for success.

Because if we just say, *"I want you to do this, I want you to do that,"* we're just throwing tasks to the Virtual Assistant without showing the process behind those tasks, the thoughts behind those tasks, the consequences if they don't do it or the consequences if they do it, we're not helping the Virtual Assistants to help us.

When you are delegating to a local team member, they have you right there. They can always come into your office and ask you a quick question. They can hear you speak to clients and learn from you directly. But a virtual team does not have that privilege. They are not across the whole business. They most likely are not up to date with all the latest things that happen in the business. And this is because we didn't provide that information to them.

Delegating is showing, supporting, and letting go. So you show what to do, you support the Virtual Assistant to do it, you ask and answer questions, and then you let them make the mistakes. And eventually, they will learn from it. In the beginning, I taught my VA by doing the work on a *Zoom* call. For example, task number one, which is onboarding a client. When there's a new client, this is what I do: I take the information from here, I put it together, I write this message, I send it, I put the name into this report, and so on. So, I'll do that task while my VA watches it and records it. Then, my Virtual Assistant will go away and write an SOP or procedure. And then, from the SOP, next time that we need to onboard a client, we'll jump on a *Zoom* call again. Now, my Virtual Assistant will do the onboarding, and I watch them and check the procedure.

Note to self: Eliminate Self-Limitation. *Stop being constrained by thinking you have to do everything yourself. Leveraging the skills of others expands what's possible.*

Onboarding New Clients: A Client's Perspective

One of my clients recently shared how chaotic her onboarding process has been, and it really highlighted a common challenge many business owners face:

She said, *"Yep, onboarding new clients. One thing I haven't had a chance to do is create a proper process. It's been so ad hoc.*

I'm almost borderline embarrassed about how I do it, but I just keep everything in my head. When I onboard a client, I just resend the same emails over and over. I explain what we need from them and how it works, but I'd love a bit of a manual or template created. That way, when a new client comes on, they can receive a proper welcome and know exactly what we need from them."

I get it. So many of us start like this – managing everything in our heads and thinking we can handle it all. But eventually, it becomes overwhelming.

I shared with her how my VAs manage the onboarding for me, keeping everything organised in spreadsheets. I told her, *"For my VAs, they track everything–client name, status (active or cancelled), VA name, handover dates, meet-and-greet notes, where the client is based, and when they started with us. Everything is organised and managed by my VAs, so I can see it all in one place, without worrying about manually sending emails or missing details."*

This example shows how a streamlined onboarding process, supported by a Virtual Assistant, can save time and reduce stress. Instead of reinventing the wheel with every new client, you can have a system in place that ensures consistency and professionalism from the start.

Note to self: Overcoming Control Issues. *Trusting others with tasks is essential for growth.*

Once we have done this task a few times, and I know that the Virtual Assistant now gets this task and can adapt to different scenarios and different possibilities, the task is successfully delegated.

Now, obviously, there is a psychological barrier to delegation, and I'm going to show you how to overcome those barriers because we all have them; we are human, and it's really hard to go from working with ourselves to now working with someone. So congratulations, first and foremost, on getting the business to where you have taken it. You can finally afford a Virtual Assistant, someone to help you and support you. We don't stop enough and congratulate ourselves on the hard work that we've done. So well done, congratulations!!!!

Time for a change...

Now is the time to change and get your life back. If you want to work less, if you want to keep making the same amount of money by working less hours, if you don't want to work on weekends, if you don't want to work evenings, and if you want to spend time with your family... It's time to change!

Change carries a lot of resistance. It's normal. We're human beings. We're creatures of habit. We like to do things the same way. I read an incredible book on change and I ask all my VA's to read it. It's called *Who Moved My Cheese* by Dr. Spencer Johnson. It's a really good book that tells you the story about change, who accepted it and who refused to go with it. It's the same in our business. If we keep doing things the same way, we're not going to get the business to the next level. We will not get to a future version of ourselves. We will not meet our full potential. We will not see what we can achieve.

- Every change can be challenging, but it's not impossible. Are you willing to be uncomfortable for a little while for you to get your time back? YES OR NO

- Are you willing to be stretched for a little while to finally have your time back? YES OR NO

- Are you willing to take yourself out of your comfort zone for you to really get your time back? YES OR NO

It's not impossible. It's possible.

Listen, it's not going to be easy. Your team is not going to do the tasks as perfectly as you probably do because they don't have the years of experience that you do. They don't have the knowledge that you have. So, it's going to take a transition period. It's going to take time for your Virtual Assistant to do things to the level that you have been doing it. But progress is better than perfection. If you never start to delegate, your VA will never get there.

Note to self: Let Go of Perfectionism: *You don't have to be the one to do everything perfectly.*

And so it's about letting go of our old identity and stepping into our future self, the CEO version of us. It's a process. It's not easy. And every time there's going to be an obstacle, our brain is going to suggest *it's faster if I just do it. This is a waste of time.* And I know that the brain is going to say that, but we need to really get clear on how much our time is worth. If you multiply that by all the hours that you're not delegating, you will soon be able to see that by not delegating, you're wasting a lot of money. So, you need to let go of your old identity.

We all have different hats. We have the marketing hat, the sales hat, the customer service hat, the admin hat, the bookkeeping hat, and so many more different hats. We cannot keep holding on to all the hats if we want the business to go to the next level. It's overwhelming, and it's very stressful to handle all areas of our business. It's time for us to let go of some of them. And the only version of yourself that we will accept is the CEO version of you.

We know it will not be easy, but hey, it's not meant to be easy. If it was easy, everybody would run a business successfully. And we know for sure that most businesses never get to the million-dollar threshold. As per a research, only 5% of businesses get to $2 million. And that is because 95% of people are unwilling to let go. They're not willing to watch other people do things and make mistakes. There's only 5% of people who are willing and have successfully delegated to get to the seven-figure business and beyond.

The question is, are you one of those people? Are you one of the 5%?

You need to be patient and remember that your future self will love you for this decision. Every time there's a challenge, every time there's a difficulty, every time it's going to be frustrating, and every time that you are going to doubt the process, go back to your future self and have an imaginary conversation with your future you … I mean that future self of yours that is by the pool on a holiday while the virtual team works behind the scenes, right? That's the version of you that you want to get to, right?

Are you inspired by your future self? Does it motivate you to take those steps that are difficult, scary, and challenging, even when you don't know how? Despite the fear and uncertainty, are you still committed to becoming that future version of yourself? Here's a very good exercise for you to do to get clear on your future goal and be clear on where you want to be.

- Do you still want to work 9am to 5pm - 5 days a week, or
- Do you want to have 20 people working for you while you are on holiday for four months of the year?

There's nothing that can stop you, well the only thing that can stop you is your brain, your fear, and your doubt.

And of course I know it because I was there… doing this exercise at a course and after having an imaginary conversation with my future self, I froze. My brain kept asking how it was going to be possible? My brain kept wanting to know the HOW to believe it was going to happen… But the HOW is not important. Right now, all you need to do is close your eyes and imagine your future self… ask him/her questions, stay curious and even if it feels weird keep going with it. I promise you it works!

That's how I've done it. I imagined working 10-15 hours a week while my team would wow our clients. I imagined reaching 100 VA's and nine staff members working full time for our business and BOOM! We nearly got there! In just over two years in this new business, we now have seven full-time Virtual Assistants. We are about to hire two more. So, we're going to have nine full-time

Virtual Assistants that work solely in my business and then we have over 60 Virtual Assistants that work for our clients. So, we are managing over 70 people in our business at the moment while I am working 15 hours a week.

And this is happening because I was willing to connect to my future self and I was so excited to get there fast!

I am living my future self's version and that is thanks to the leap of faith I took of hiring VA's to help me.

My Realisations

What I learned when I started my business as a one-person team, doing everything myself, was that I got quick at doing many tasks. But let's be real: as the business grew, I had less time to spend on *Canva*. I had to focus on social media to grow the business. What people say about holding on too long to certain tasks happened to me. And if this happens to you too, you have two choices: either you become inconsistent with a strategy that works, or you keep it up. I've seen it many times–people are active on social media, then stop because they run out of time. Suddenly, they realise their business isn't growing, so they rush back to social media. Then, just as things pick up again, they stop once more to support their new clients. It becomes a cycle, and this is where you get tired, burned out, and overwhelmed. That roller coaster of strategy will also be a rollercoaster of your finances. Because if you don't have consistency in your marketing, you will not have consistency in your cash flow.

And the other thing that is going to happen if you keep doing everything is that you're going to burnout. I was doing an okay job.

But when my Virtual Assistant began marketing full time, and all they were doing every day was social media, writing content, blogs, and *Canva*, they became amazing at it. So now, it's not faster if I do it anymore; it's faster if they do it because they became an expert. And I was never an expert. I was only doing it well enough.

I always say to my clients, and I always say this to myself: whatever got me here will never get me there. So, if I've got a clear future version of myself, I need to let go of the way that I've done things and allow things to change so I can go to the next level.

If you have a bad experience, you can't just give up. When you give up on hiring people, you're essentially giving up on the future version of yourself. Is that something you're truly willing to do? Are you prepared to give up on the lifestyle-business you've always dreamed of or the time you wanted to spend with your family? What are you really willing to sacrifice instead of delegating? That's the real question. There will always be consequences if you don't delegate, and you need to consider what those consequences are before making that decision.

It will save you time in the long run. But you will have to invest time in the first three months. Hiring a Virtual Assistant will feel like a waste of time in the first three months. And because every beginning is hard, we have to spend time with our team to train them, support them, teach them, and show them how things are done. No matter where you get your Virtual Assistant from. And this is not just for Virtual Assistants, it's for any new staff member.

Note to self: Avoid Burnout. Avoid burnout by delegating tasks that don't energise you.

Just today, I spoke with a client who said, *"I have an event in two weeks, and I'm hiring a Virtual Assistant for that short time to fill up my event! I'm so excited because if they don't fill it up, they won't be hired."*

The expectation placed on this VA was unrealistically high. They were given two weeks to prove they can bring in business or lose the job. But let's be honest: even if you hire someone for a $100,000 salary, they won't bring in business immediately. It could take three, four, or even six months before you see any real results. We need to be realistic with our expectations of our team members so we can set them up for success, not set them up for failure. In the first few months, they probably won't save you time; in fact, they might take more of your time. But the long-term payoff is that they will free up your time for the rest of your life!

Now, my questions to you...

- Are you willing to 'suffer' short term?
- Are you willing to spend the time and the energy with your VA and really be focused on their onboarding?

You may experience a temporary setback in your cash flow when you dedicate more time to training, resulting in a slight decline in business momentum. It's part of the journey, but you need to keep focusing on what's going to happen after the three months. How much time you're going to get back, and how much money you can make when you have all that time back.

Once your VA is fully trained, and you can finally take all those tasks off your plate, the question becomes: what could you achieve with all that extra time? Yes, it's going to be time-consuming in those first three months, but the payoff will be huge. You won't just get your time back – you'll have the potential to grow your business exponentially, whether that means doubling, tripling, or even quadrupling your results. After that initial three-month investment, you'll be able to focus fully on the big-picture goals and truly make your vision happen.

It takes a lot of trust and faith to allow someone else to take over. But what is the option here? What if you don't have trust? What if you don't have faith? Are you willing to work as you've been working for the rest of your life? Because for me it was a no brainer. I'd rather delegate and have the pain of delegation than have to work 24/7 for the rest of my life.

We need to focus on pinpointing the tasks that are ripe for delegation. It's essential to distinguish between high-value tasks and those time-consuming tasks that you really should hand over to your Virtual Assistant. I've developed a simple rule to help my clients figure out what they need to delegate versus what they need to handle personally.

Here's the rule: The CEO should do things just once. Here's what that means – whenever I do something, I always consider whether I'll need to do it again. If it's likely to recur, then I need to develop a procedure, make a template, and delegate it to my Virtual Assistant. However, if it's a one-off task, something unique that I won't repeat, then it's probably something I should manage directly. For example, a sales call is something I prefer to engage in myself because it's often a one-time interaction with a client.

For any task that's repetitive, we need to create a procedure and pass it onto the Virtual Assistant. Delegating tasks I do more than once is crucial because it's all about valuing our time – both mine and yours. That's why I've created a CEO checklist. This tool helps you identify the current tasks in your business, especially those that are too time-consuming for you to continue handling.

In this CEO checklist, there's a section to note how much time each task takes you every week. There's also a column for tasks that your business needs to accomplish but currently, no one has the time or energy to take on, so they just don't get done. For instance, writing a blog could be beneficial for the business, but if it's always been on your wish list and never done because you don't have the time– it's not a priority.

After you fill out this checklist, you'll see the total hours you're currently working and the total hours you should delegate. You'll also identify how many hours your business needs someone to do something that's currently being neglected. Once you see the figures, you'll realise, *"Oh my gosh, I need someone for 40 hours a week to take things off my shoulders and also to tackle the tasks that will help grow the business."*

We've also developed a simple valuation table to help you grasp the true worth of your time, because often, we tell ourselves, *it's quicker if I just do it myself. It's only 15 minutes, or just an hour. I can handle it while binge-watching Netflix tonight.* But the real issue isn't about how quickly you can do the task; it's about valuing your time properly.

Using the template I've created, you can calculate your hourly rate, which should be at least $400. Our PDF will make it clear why you should delegate at least 20 hours of your weekly tasks. The math is straightforward: 20 hours multiplied by $400 per hour equals $8,000. That's $8,000 a week you're essentially wasting by handling tasks that aren't the best use of your time. It's like throwing $8,000 into the trash every week.

So, it's crucial to identify the tasks you need to delegate and learn how to delegate effectively to potentially double your business. As a CEO, you must focus on what truly matters. Ask yourself:

What is the one task or department you should spend most of your week on to drive your business forward?

- Administration?
- Customer service?
- Marketing?
- Business development?
- Sales?

Likely, you should be spending about 80% of your time on sales activities, 10% on marketing, and the remaining 10% on delegation. Yet often, we find ourselves doing the exact opposite.

We get bogged down with administrative tasks, reacting rather than acting, which consumes 80% of our time. We focus too little on what truly drives our business forward - the money making activities. These should occupy the largest portion of our calendar, not the smallest.

If you're a coach, a significant portion of your time will obviously be devoted to coaching clients. However, even this should not dominate your schedule.

A Virtual Assistant is invaluable for handling the tasks you lack the time or energy for. Whether it's admin, customer service, social media, managing your calendar, or handling emails, VAs are the backbone of your business operations. They implement the strategies and groundwork that you lay out. They're not strategists or marketers–they are your implementation team.

I've often been asked, *"Should I hire a marketing manager here in Australia full-time or a Virtual Assistant?"* This shouldn't even be a question.

It's really interesting how often people find themselves pondering, *"Should I do this or that?"* No, if you lack the strategy, find someone who can provide it, then let a VA execute it. Many of us have business goals that remain unmet, likely because we're too caught up reacting to the day-to-day demands.

You might find yourself exhausted and burned out, thinking, *I can't handle this anymore.* Yet you continue to juggle endless tasks. Maybe you're disorganised, merely reacting to whatever the business throws your way, or perhaps you've been disillusioned by past hiring experiences. So, you decide to do it alone. You think *I'm done hiring. I'll just handle everything myself,* or *I've tried delegating before; it didn't work out, and I don't want to waste my time again.* Sometimes, it's a mix of all these feelings.

Investing in your business is essential. To see growth, you must invest–whether that's in paid advertising, hiring staff, or engaging a coach. Consider where and how to invest:

- How much should you invest?
- How will you recoup that investment?
- What's your timeline for seeing a return?

Planning these investments carefully is key to moving forward and achieving those elusive business goals.

3 MAIN BENEFITS OF HIRING A VA

Hiring a Virtual Assistant will do three things:

- Save us time.
- Save us money.
- Make us money.

Many people have the misconception that hiring a Virtual Assistant will make money. No, the VA will save you time so that you can make more money. The VA is not the one making sales calls. If you hire a VA in marketing, they will help you get more leads. They will help you be seen more on social media. They will help you do all the administration tasks but they will not help you to actually sell. Eventually, they will. I've got VAs; they've been with me for years now, and they make me money.

They actually sell products on my social media like the Time Management Course - we sell those small ticket items every week. So those are sold by my Virtual Assistants on social media, but before, when I didn't have a very strong following, there was no money making from my Virtual Assistant, but they brought me leads and then it's my job to actually do the sales call.

The most effective way to a sustainable and scalable business is for us to create a business that runs without us and for us to do that, we need to learn how to delegate and what to delegate.

It's really important to identify the tasks Virtual Assistants should NOT spend time in?

- Sales calls
- Content creation - recording videos (The VA can't record for us)
- Collaboration
- Networking
- Coaching your clients
- Reviewing business reports
- Approving content
- Reviewing Financial reports

Those are the areas where you should really focus your energy. Everything else? Let your Virtual Assistant handle it. Imagine you're the CEO of your business that's already pulling in $1 million, and now you're looking to hire another CEO because you want to take a holiday with your family.

You're conducting interviews and one candidate comes in and says, *"I'm your dream CEO. You won't need to hire anyone else, no Virtual Assistants, nobody. I can handle everything from Canva graphics to complex strategies. Just pay me $200,000 a year, and I'll do it all. I'm great at multitasking. I can manage social media, create graphics, draft content, close sales, run marketing – everything."* Would you really hire this person? Would you pay someone $200,000 to spend their time on tasks like designing in *Canva*? I hope you won't.

A friend of mine once said, *"Francesca, I don't mind doing my bookkeeping at night while watching Netflix."* I told them, *"You should be relaxing, letting an expert handle the bookkeeping so you can focus on making sales the next day. Don't burn yourself out thinking you have to do it all."*

Never hire a multitasking CEO. If you were to assess your own performance as a CEO, based on how you spend your week, you might find you'd fire yourself. Ideally, a CEO should focus solely on delegating and driving sales, not getting bogged down in day-to-day operations.

It's crucial to recognise if you're spending hours on tasks that don't propel business growth, if you're tight on funds, it's likely because you're too caught up in admin, customer service, or backend tasks that don't directly contribute to your bottom line.

The golden rule? If a task needs to be done more than once, create a procedure for it and delegate it. The focus should be on activities that truly require the CEO's touch–like sales calls, recording videos for marketing content, engaging with leads, or networking. These are tasks that your Virtual Assistants can't replicate.

Everything else should be delegated. It's not just a smart move; it's enjoyable too.

Time is money, and every hour you spend on non-essential tasks is money down the drain. It's vital to calculate the true cost of your time. Can you justify spending $3,800 a week on something you could delegate for far less?

To help you see what tasks are typically delegated, I've included here a PDF called **100 Tasks You Should Delegate to a Virtual Assistant**. This guide will show you what other clients are outsourcing to their VAs, helping you understand how to effectively lighten your load and focus on what truly matters.

We want to encourage you to fully envision your future self. Understand your goals and dreams and align your daily actions with that vision.

Imagine yourself not as someone who's stuck in front of a computer day in and day out, but as someone who works efficiently—only 20 hours a week, taking long weekends off every month. Whatever your vision is, get clear about it. What does your future self look like? What are your aspirations for your business? This clarity will direct every step you take.

Once you have that vision firmly in mind, take a detailed inventory of what you do every day, every week, every month, and even annually. Identify the activities that are consuming your time without adding value. Determine what you need to stop doing immediately. Reviewing your daily tasks through the lens of your CEO responsibilities will clarify which activities are truly worth your time and which should be handed off. By doing this, managing your responsibilities becomes much simpler and more aligned with your ultimate business goals.

Check out the 100 Tasks PDF here:

Check out the CEO's VA Checklist here:

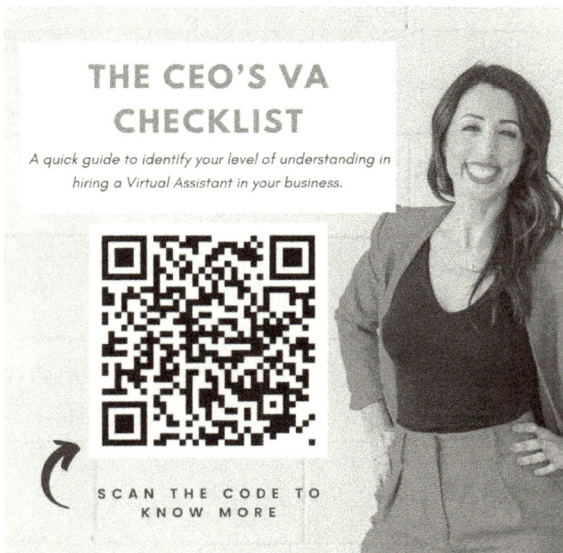

Key Takeaways:

- Delegation is crucial for reducing overwhelm, stress and burnout in running a business. It's important to overcome psychological barriers to delegation.
- Delegating tasks to a Virtual Assistant (VA) can free up time and allow business growth, but it requires a process of showing, supporting, and letting go. Micromanaging the VA hinders productivity.
- Letting go of old identities and embracing the CEO mindset is essential for effective delegation and business expansion. Connecting with your future self can help overcome delegation challenges.
- Consistency in business strategies like marketing is important, and delegation can prevent inconsistency caused by trying to do everything yourself.
- Investing time in training VAs in the first three months may not yield immediate results, but it's crucial for long-term success. Unrealistic expectations can lead to disappointment.
- Calculating the time value of your work and the cost of not delegating can motivate effective delegation. Providing a list of 100 tasks to delegate to a VA can also be helpful.
- Clarity on future business goals and vision is important to align delegation efforts with the desired future state of the business.
- TIME IS MONEY
- Setting clear boundaries on what tasks you should delegate and tasks you should keep as a CEO is a GAME-CHANGER!
- Expecting unrealistic ROI from your VA in the first month is a big NO-NO!

What actions are you going to take from this chapter?

1 _____

_____

_____

_____

_____

2 _____

_____

_____

_____

3 _____

_____

_____

_____

CHAPTER 3

MANAGING AN
ONLINE TEAM

∞

To be ready to run a business successfully with an online team, we have to be prepared for the change. We have to be aware that it's not the same as hiring a local team member as they are not in the room with you, therefore, we need to have an online proof business.

We have to know, as CEO, how to manage a team online and how to deal with conflict in between the team.

For example, every time there is a new online member, there is resistance. It's harder to build trust and build a relationship between team members, and we need to facilitate that.

1. Include online team members in ALL business meetings.
2. Monitor team conversations on slack and intervene if someone is being rude or tough with an online team member.

3. Do regular huddles to ensure the online team member doesn't feel alone

Let's go in depth in the above suggestions:

1. Include online team members in ALL business meetings. Invite your online team member in EVERY team meeting you have. Have the computer open on *Zoom* and allow your online team member to interact and speak and give you updates and present on reports.
Excluding team members, especially the VAs, can lead to a loss of interest in the business and company. And we all know that when someone loses interest, they are more prone to make mistakes or to even quit.

   People need to feel part of something to stay interested. You need to create a culture that they are proud to be part of. Celebrate their birthdays, sing a song together, give them a day off when they have achieved something, send them a voucher to spend in their favourite store. Look after them and they will look after your business.

2. Monitor team conversations on slack and intervene if someone is being rude or tough with an online team member.

   I have set up my slack channels in different departments and every couple of hours I spend five minutes reading what's going on in the business. If I had all my staff in the office, I would hear what is going on with my team, I would hear their conversation with clients over the phone. I would hear the conversations between my team members. As my team is online, I don't have that privilege, so I found a way to be present and be across the business.

3. Do regular huddles to ensure the online team member doesn't feel alone. Huddles are a brief chat over *Slack* to ensure we are on the same page. I do it while I drive to the office, it also helps me to be in business mode. I have to be careful as I am a creative business owner (I will tell you more about business owner personality types in the next chapter) so that I can go on tangents and waste my VAs time with my crazy ideas.

In chapter 10, I will discuss more about the most common mistake business owners make with their virtual team.

Preparing For A Virtual Assistant

Note to self: Hire a VA before you drown.

One thing that I hear a lot of people say is, *"I am not ready for a Virtual Assistant."*

Let me share with you the five signs that you are ready for a Virtual Assistant right now. Deep down you know you are ready, but your brain is saying that you *don't know where to start and it's easier to just keep going and working on your own.*

So, here are the five signs WHY you should hire a VA before you drown:

1. Working 24/7?

If you're constantly glued to your computer, working around the clock, and always on your phone and managing emails, it's time to delegate those time-consuming tasks, by creating a template and a procedure so that your VA can easily take over those tasks. And if you think you are the only person who can do those, remember most tasks can be delegated. I'm living proof of that. You know, a recovering control freak. lol

2. Wearing too many hats?

If you are handling marketing, sales, admin, and bookkeeping all alone or all at once… You're stretching yourself too thin. Usually, when business owners wear many hats, they find themselves overwhelmed and procrastinating because they just simply cannot do it all! It's humanly impossible, and it's not the best use of your time. Trust me, I've been there too!

It's time to delegate.

Note to self: Maximise Your Unique Abilities. Focus on what you're uniquely good at and passionate about. Delegate the rest to those whose strengths complement yours.

3. Ghosting your own clients?

Are you finding yourself so busy that you take ages to get back to your clients' or prospects' emails, requests, or messages because you simply don't have the time to get back to everyone in your ideal time frame? I hear you. This is a huge sign that you need a VA asap. We usually say hire a VA before you drown, and you might be drowning already. But if you are, the answer is not to continue drowning until it gets better, because it will never get better until you offload some tasks. And this is where our 'Quick Replies Template' comes in so that your VA can easily reply for you, while still sticking to your brand voice.

4. Sales Neglected?

When you are focusing most of your week on backend tasks, your business will suffer because you are not focusing your energy on sales. You must prioritise revenue-generating activities. You cannot do that if you are stuck in the back end. So let me ask you a question: how many more clients could you bring in if you had twenty hours back? Don't wait any longer. It's time!

5. When was your last holiday??

Can't remember your last holiday? You're overdue for a breather. We always think we don't have time for a holiday, but if you keep pushing, you are going to burn out, and then your business will really suffer. I've noticed that after a holiday, my energy towards my clients, business, and team improves significantly.

When I am due for a holiday, I feel resentful towards the business, and I don't have time to show up as my best self. If you are resonating with this, be kind to yourself and get a break. You deserve it! And your team will be grateful you took the break.

And if you are thinking to yourself: *I cannot go on holidays because the business will fall apart*, then this is another super important reason for you to delegate and gain your life back! I promise you, it's possible to delegate and go on a holiday. Having a VA that will hold the fort for you while you enjoy your me-time is sooooo worth it!

And we can help you find an incredible VA so you can relax.

*Note to self: **Multiply Time and Productivity**. Delegating frees up time, allowing you to focus on strategic, high-value activities.*

If you're exhausted from working non-stop, if you truly need a holiday because you deserve one, and if you're ready to start managing someone instead of doing everything yourself, then it's time to focus on securing consistent clients and sales. If you've managed to achieve consistent sales and clients in the past few months, you're definitely ready for a Virtual Assistant. A VA can help you maintain balance and efficiency, ensuring you have the support needed to grow your business and enjoy the benefits of having someone else handle tasks, giving you time to recharge. Remember, there will never be the perfect time to hire someone, much like there's never a perfect time to have kids. If people waited until they were fully ready, the world would be a very different place. Hire someone to help you now and figure out the rest along the way. You can do this!

I just spoke with a client who owns a hair salon. She expressed frustration over how her clients were coming in inconsistently. When she finds the time, she does marketing, which brings in clients, but then she becomes busy servicing these clients, she stops marketing, and when the initial rush ends, she's back to square one with no more clients and must start all over! If this situation sounds familiar, remember—you're not superhuman. This is a common pattern for those trying to do it all alone. When you stop marketing, the leads dry up, and once you've attended to all your clients and return to marketing, you're left wondering, *"Where are the leads?"* You find yourself starting from scratch each time. To break this endless cycle, it's crucial to maintain a steady marketing effort. You must delegate your marketing tasks to ensure you don't lose momentum and can continuously attract new clients while managing the existing ones effectively.

*Note to self: **Time is Limited.*** *You cannot scale your time, but you can scale your impact through others.*

Conducting your time audit...

*Note to self: **Energy vs. Money.*** *Prioritise tasks that give you energy over those that just save money.*

Many business coaches advise business owners to list every single task they spend time on throughout their day, but most people don't follow through. For you to understand what to delegate, we need to consider a few things:

1. Identify tasks you should not be doing yourself and should delegate.
2. Determine tasks that your business needs done, but no one currently has time to do.
3. Decide what tasks your team should delegate.

As I mentioned before, I recommend my clients to keep in mind that us or the manager should ONLY keep tasks that need to be done ONCE. Anything that is repetitive MUST be delegated.

Many business owners don't know how much time each task takes, which is why we have created the 'Brainstorm of Tasks File'. This resource includes examples of the most common tasks our clients are currently delegating to their Virtual Assistants and provides an average time each task takes. This will help you better understand where your efforts should be focused and what can be handed off to a VA to make your operations more efficient. We will go more in depth about the Brainstorm of tasks in chapter 5.

The Power of Delegation

	Admin	Count 9	Sum 11.5
1	Email Management inbox		1.5
2	Data Entry (Collating of information, or uploading information into spreadsheets or Database)		1.5
3	Calendar Management/Appointment Setting		1.5
☐	CRM Management (keep the CRM tidy)		2.0
5	Filing of Digital Assets (File photos and videos and docs into your DB or GD)		1.0
6	Meeting time		1.5
7	Daily Reporting / weekly reporting		1.0
8	Team Communication and updates (slack)		1.0
9	Planning (montly + quaterly meeting)		0.5

AREA
	Customer Service	Count 5	Sum 4.5
10	Helpdesk & Liaising with clients (Receptionist Services + Email and Chat Support)		1.0
11	Onboarding new clients		1.0
12	Nurturing of current clients and managing clients reports		1.5
13	Manage Client Contracts		0.5
14	Ask clients for reviews and testimonials		0.5

AREA
	Marketing	Count 14	Sum 33.5
15	Content Calendar Management: Social Media scheduling & posting #7/week (posting, sharin...		3.0
16	Social Media creation (# 5/week captions, content, graphics on canva)		3.5
17	Connect with Potential Leads (FB/IG/LinkedIn) + Booking sales calls from HOT leads		3.5
18	Social Media Management: Engage in Social Media Groups / Replying to comments		1.5
19	Own FB Group Community Manager		1.0
20	Video Editing and reels creation (2 reels) + Audio Transcription		5.0
☐	Lead Generation (Collecting Emails, lead magnet creation)		2.5
22	Email Marketing		2.0
23	Website Maintenance (Updating website + landing pages)		3.0
24	Sales Pipeline management		1.5
25	Market reseach		3.0
26	Automation		1.0
27	Support on online Masterclasses		1.5
28	Product Development		1.5

AREA
	Finance	Count 5	Sum 2.5
29	Basic Bookkeeping (invoicing)		0.5
30	Chasing up invoices		0.5
31	Payment reminders		0.5
32	Creating invoices		0.5
33	xero		0.5

AREA
	Operations	Count 1	Sum 1.5
34	Updating of Business Procedures		1.5

AREA
	Projects	Count 2	Sum 4.5
35	Project Management		2.0
36	Working on Ongoing Projects		2.5

We want you to fill out tasks that can be delegated to a Virtual Assistant and note how much time these tasks take each week. This is part of the brainstorming tasks file. We encourage you to fill it out completely. If you wish, you can also book a call with one of my team members for a game-changer call, which we offer free of charge to all our clients and to you, the reader. When we review this list together, you'll gain a clear understanding of exactly what you can delegate to a Virtual Assistant. Through this process, you'll learn how to delegate tasks to your VA and where to best spend your time in the business.

If you think you're not ready for a Virtual Assistant, remember, you'll never feel fully prepared. There's never a 'right' time. It's like having children—nobody is ever truly ready for the change it brings, yet somehow, we manage. Hiring someone is similar. You're unlikely to find someone in three months where you're just waiting around because if you do, it probably means you don't have enough business. Hiring requires juggling things initially, but that's how you free up time eventually. Bringing someone new onto the team requires an upfront investment of effort and time, but the long-term payoff is significant. By distributing the workload, you allow your business to expand and provide yourself the chance to focus on strategic tasks, ultimately leading to increased efficiency and success.

GOALS AND EXPECTATIONS

Clear goals and expectations are crucial. After conducting a time audit and clarifying our goals and expectations around delegation, we need a detailed delegation plan. For instance, for a Marketing VA, we might set the objective to generate 200 new leads each month, convert 20 of these into calls, and secure ten new clients from those calls.

Once these targets, or KPIs, are set, we can outline a plan for our Virtual Assistant to achieve these results, ensuring they're a valuable long-term member of the team.

If a VA fails to meet a KPI, the response shouldn't be immediate dismissal. Instead, engage in a constructive dialogue: *"You haven't reached your KPI this month, let's explore why."* Together, we can adjust the marketing strategy to improve outcomes for the following month. Providing this support is essential for helping them meet their goals.

Regrettably, many business owners neglect regular checks on KPI reports, leading to frustration over poor results. As the saying goes, *"Doers don't do what checkers don't check."* As CEOs, we are the checkers, and the VAs are the doers–it's our responsibility to monitor their performance to ensure desired outcomes.

Successful delegation will give you your life back. Imagine leaving the office at five without a backward glance, enjoying weekends with your family, knowing the business continues to thrive, generating consistent leads, and functioning efficiently, even in your absence.

If your VA is managing admin tasks effectively, you'll know because you'll reclaim more of your time. Consistent business operations without your direct involvement indicate successful marketing task delegation. These signs show that you've delegated well, allowing you to focus on strategic growth activities rather than day-to-day operations, balancing your workload to enhance productivity and growth.

So ask yourself, *"If I take a week off, what will I return to? A backlog of tasks? Will I need to work overtime to catch up, or will everything run smoothly?"* Your answers will reveal whether your business setup truly supports your freedom or if you're still enslaved by it–a harsh reality I faced for seven years. Although I had many team members, my business overly depended on me. Now, freedom is mine because I've empowered my team with proper procedures, a journey I detail in Chapter 8.

Do you need a VA Part Time or Full Time?

After determining your needs for a Virtual Assistant through the brainstorming tasks previously discussed, it's crucial to decide if you require 20 or 40 hours of assistance per week. I don't advocate for employing a Virtual Assistant on a casual or ad hoc basis. This approach often fails to work in the long term. Typically, VAs working casually aren't fully committed to your business because they manage several others simultaneously. They may disappear for days or weeks as they focus on different projects, resulting in unreliability. This is why people often say, *"it's faster if I just do it myself."* If you've had experiences with casually employing people, you've likely found that the time spent explaining your brand and instructing them on their tasks could have been spent doing the work yourself. For these reasons, I recommend hiring someone for at least 20 hours a week.

The benefits of having a Virtual Assistant, whether part-time or full-time are significant. Full-time engagement is my preferred arrangement and here's why: it allows you to develop a trusting relationship where you can confidently delegate tasks. Initially, you'll need to provide some guidance, but once a VA is up to speed, they become an integral part of your operations. I often ask my VAs, *"Hey, where's that PowerPoint we created four years ago?"* They're adept at navigating our business's backend–finding things I didn't even remember we had.

When VAs work full-time, they are entirely devoted to your business. Training them is quicker because they aren't juggling multiple clients and can focus solely on your preferences and processes. They're all yours. If an urgent issue arises, you can readily have them join a *Zoom* call during their shift. This immediacy isn't feasible when they are split between different businesses.

It's essential for someone to work consistently within your business rather than on a casual basis. This consistency builds trust, allowing you to delegate increasingly complex tasks over time. They grow to understand your business intimately–its goals and operations–enabling them to handle substantial responsibilities with confidence. This deep familiarity allows you to focus on strategic growth, securely knowing that your VA is competently managing day-to-day tasks.

Pros and cons of part-time and full-time...
When we hire Virtual Assistants part-time, training them becomes a more prolonged process because they work four hours a day instead of eight. During those other four hours, they're likely working for someone else, which means they're juggling mixed information, branding, messages, and procedures. This division of attention can make it challenging for them to commit fully to your business. After their four-hour shift is up, that's it–they're off to their next job.

In contrast, when someone works full-time in your business, their entire focus is on you and your operations. Everything they do is about contributing effectively to your business. For me, having someone full-time is incredibly valuable. It's really a matter of cash flow. Some people opt for part-time because they believe full-time isn't financially feasible. However, every time I've hired someone part-time, it has backfired. It's harder to build a relationship, train them, and for them to retain information. Repetition is the mother of skill; the more time and energy someone dedicates to your business, the quicker they learn and integrate into your team. I always prefer full-time engagement. Cash flow concerns often lead businesses to start with part-time roles, but transitioning to full-time should be a goal as soon as it's viable.

It's crucial to set clear objectives and expectations with a Virtual Assistant. It's not just about hiring someone to fill 40 hours and then sending them off on their own. Learning the tasks and skills necessary to effectively fill those hours takes time and doesn't happen instantly.

In our business, when a new Virtual Assistant starts, their first task is a meeting with their supervisor to breakdown their primary tasks into three manageable phases. We start with phase one, which typically includes the most recurring and simpler tasks. This approach prevents overwhelming the VA at the start. If we throw all tasks at them all at once, it can be too much and hinder their effectiveness.

Our goal is to see long-term results and maximise the VA's role, so we divide the training into three phases. This gradual integration helps build confidence that the VA will learn step-by-step. After about three months, we can usually tell if the person is a keeper–they've got it.

We follow the principle: 'hire slow, fire fast.' This approach means that if someone isn't performing well, it becomes apparent early on, especially if we haven't burdened them with an overload of tasks. By dividing tasks into phases, focusing on one thing at a time, and using our delegation fast track protocol, we can accurately determine if a Virtual Assistant will thrive as a valuable asset in our team or if they're not the right fit for our business.

Key Takeaways...

- Make sure your business is fully set up to run online before hiring remote team members.
- As the CEO, it's crucial to know how to handle any issues or conflicts that arise within your remote team.
- New online hires may face resistance from existing team members. Focus on building trust and easing that transition.
- Always invite your remote team members to all business meetings. This makes them feel like part of the team and keeps them engaged.
- Check in on team communications, like *Slack*, to ensure everyone's treating each other respectfully, especially remote members.
- Regular, casual check-ins can make a huge difference in helping your remote team members feel included and supported.
- Celebrate your remote team's wins, acknowledge their birthdays, and show them they matter. It goes a long way in keeping them motivated.
- Delegating is important, but it's just as vital to monitor progress. Set clear expectations and check in regularly to ensure success.
- Avoid letting your remote team members feel like they're on an island. Keep them involved in daily operations and discussions.
- Be mindful of staying on track during meetings–don't let your creativity sidetrack your team and waste valuable time.

What actions are you going
to take from this chapter?

1 _____

_____

_____

_____

_____

2 _____

_____

_____

_____

3 _____

_____

_____

_____

CHAPTER 4

HIRING YOUR VIRTUAL ASSISTANT

∞

Now that you understand you want a Virtual Assistant, that you need a Virtual Assistant, and your business deserves a Virtual Assistant, and that there is no reason for you to work 24/7, what's next?

Understanding YOU is a must... What type of Business Owner are you?

I love learning about myself. It helps me to recognise my strengths and my weaknesses, and to improve the things that don't come naturally to me and to delegate the things I am terrible at. Before I took time to understand myself, I would be so harsh with myself, but since I have clarity, I can use my strengths to my advantage.

In the world of entrepreneurship, no two business owners are alike. However, most entrepreneurs align with one of three distinct business owner types: the Creator, the Leader, and the Business Savvy. Each type brings unique strengths to the table, but also comes with its own set of challenges. Understanding which type you most closely align with can help you leverage your strengths, address your weaknesses, and ultimately build a more successful and balanced business.

Three different types of business owners:

There is the Creator. Creators are the visionaries of the business world. They thrive on generating new ideas and often have a knack for innovation. Their minds are constantly buzzing with possibilities, and they have a natural ability to see opportunities where others may not. Creators are often driven by their passion and creativity, and they are always on the lookout for the next big idea.

The creators have all the ideas. Usually, these people are not very good at following through on those ideas. They get overwhelmed and struggle to implement their ideas. Some of them, sometimes, also procrastinate. They need support from someone to implement those ideas.

Pros:

- Innovative Thinking: Creators are excellent at coming up with new concepts, products, or services. Their creativity often leads to groundbreaking ideas that can set their business apart from the competition.

- Passion-Driven: Their enthusiasm for their ideas can be infectious, inspiring those around them to buy into their vision and work towards bringing it to life.
- Adaptability: Creators are often flexible and can pivot quickly if a new opportunity or idea arises.
- People Master: Very good at connecting with people and naturally sales skills.

Cons:

- Lack of Follow-Through: While they excel at idea generation, Creators often struggle with implementing those ideas. They may get easily overwhelmed by the details and lose momentum.
- Procrastination: Their tendency to juggle multiple ideas at once can lead to procrastination, making it difficult to bring projects to completion.
- Overwhelm: With so many ideas constantly swirling in their minds, Creators can quickly become overwhelmed, leading to burnout or stagnation.

How to Succeed as a Creator?

To thrive as a Creator, it's essential to build a team that complements your strengths and addresses your weaknesses. Surround yourself with individuals who excel at execution and are detail-oriented. Learn to prioritise your ideas, focusing on one or two at a time to avoid overwhelm. Additionally, developing a basic understanding of leadership and business strategy can help you bridge the gap between idea and execution.

And for a Virtual Assistant to work for a creator, it is very difficult and very frustrating at times. Often the VA just cannot keep up with us or they're just all over the place, just like us. And for us, it's important that we slow down and we commit to talk to the VA consistently. It's hard, I hear you. I know that it's hard because it's hard for me as well. But you must sit down, go to *Zoom* and chat with your VA at least once or twice a week. It's priceless. You will bring the relationship to the next level together, and you won't break your VA. (more on chapter 10 on how to avoid 'breaking' your VA).

The Leader.
The orchestrators of the business world. They are skilled at managing people and processes, and they thrive on organisation and structure. Leaders are often natural-born motivators, able to inspire and guide

their teams toward achieving business goals. They are excellent at delegation and ensuring that the right tasks are assigned to the right people.

The Leader is that person who is very good at managing people and is very good at telling other people what to do. They lack ideas, they lack business savvy, they're just more a type of leader. They can delegate, they can tell people what to do, but sometimes they struggle with ideas or struggle with ways on how to innovate and improve the business, they sort of get stuck. So the danger for that person is that they might not know how to grow the business, right? They can only get the business to a certain point.

Pros:

- Team Management: Leaders excel at building and managing teams. They understand how to delegate tasks effectively and keep everyone on track.
- Decision-Making: they are confident decision-makers, able to guide their teams through challenges and toward success.
- Consistency: Leaders bring stability to a business, ensuring that operations run smoothly and efficiently.

Cons:

- Limited Innovation: Leaders may struggle with generating new ideas or thinking outside the box. They often rely on their teams for creative input.
- Potential Stagnation: without the ability to innovate or push boundaries, leaders may find themselves stuck in a routine, unable to grow the business beyond a certain point.

- Dependence on Others: because they may lack the creative spark or business savvy, Leaders can become overly dependent on others for innovation and strategic direction.

How to Succeed as a Leader?

Leaders should focus on building a strong network of creative and strategic partners who can help them innovate and expand their business. Embracing a learning mindset and seeking out opportunities to improve their creative and business skills can also help Leaders avoid stagnation. Delegating effectively is key, but Leaders should also ensure they are not completely detached from the creative and strategic aspects of the business.

The Business savvy.

These owners are the strategists of the business world. They have a deep understanding of the mechanics of running a business, including finance, operations, and market trends. These owners are often risk-takers who are comfortable with making calculated decisions to grow their businesses. They have a keen eye for spotting profitable opportunities and are skilled at optimising resources to achieve business goals.

The business savvy is the person who has an incredible business manner. They understand numbers, they understand what's working, and what's not working. They've got the innovation, but they don't have the artistic flair that the Creator has. They have got their hands in different businesses. They're risk takers, they invest a lot of money in the business. And they just keep going.

Pros:

- Strategic Thinking: business Savvy owners excel at analysing data, identifying trends, and making informed decisions that drive growth.
- Financial Acumen: they have a strong grasp of financial management, ensuring that their businesses are profitable and sustainable.
- Risk Tolerance: these owners are not afraid to take risks, often leading to significant business opportunities and growth.

Cons:

- Lack of Creativity: while they are skilled at managing the numbers, Business Savvy owners may struggle with creative or innovative thinking, making it difficult to differentiate their business in the market.
- Limited People Skills: they may not be the best at managing people or leading a team, which can create challenges in building a cohesive and motivated workforce.
- Overextension: their willingness to take risks can sometimes lead to overextension, where they spread themselves too thin across multiple ventures or projects.

How to succeed as a business savvy?
Business Savvy owners should prioritise building a team that includes strong creative and leadership elements. This balance will ensure that the business continues to innovate and maintain a motivated workforce. Additionally, developing basic leadership and people management skills can help Business Savvy owners build a more well-rounded approach to business.

It is important for you as a business owner to understand which one you are. One view is that we have all three of them. Sometimes we want to be business savvy, but are we really? If we are honest with ourselves, we would love to be savvy people in business, but probably we're not. And you can tell from the numbers. Is your business thriving? Are you in profit? Is the financing amazing? That means you're a business savvy person. Or are you more of an artistic person who has a lot of ideas, but actually struggles to get, you know, things down, right?

At my core, I identify as a Creator. I have a plethora of ideas. I've discovered the importance of focusing on business acumen rather than creative pursuits in order to grow my business. I had to put that on hold briefly and master the art of being a leader. So I could be a better leader to my team.

When I'm stressed, I become a terrible leader and become really overwhelmed by business and about money and all of that. When we are stressed, we go back to our core.

I would like you to really have a look at that. Where are you at in your business? What does that look like? And what are the positives and negatives of your personality? The knowledge of just knowing what my strengths are, what my weaknesses are, means I can hire people around me to help me and support me. For example, I've learned how to be organised. I've learned how to be a leader. But as I said, it is not my core, it is not natural to me. I had to learn how to be organised, I had to learn to slow down to implement the most important ideas and let go of the ones that were time wasting and not going to take me closer to my goals. I had to make mistakes and learn from them.

I also know it's not my core when something drains me. It drains me to lead and be a leader, training people, managing my team and approving things. It drains me if I do it for a long time. But I still do it and I became quite good at it... as long as I can still spend time doing what I love most... coming up with ideas!!!

If I'm in business savvy mode, doing numbers and taking risks, I can do it. I've learned how to do it. But it drains me as well. So when I plan my week, I can actually go okay, I need to do all three of them because I need the business to thrive, but I need to be kind to myself. When I schedule the week, I can schedule the week in a way that supports me rather than drains me. And this is exactly what I have done, and it really helped me to create a little bit of a structure throughout my week and set myself up for success rather than failure.

As CEOs, we do things like changing our minds a lot of the time. And it's very hard for staff members to follow us and to help us.

In my Virtual Assistant agency, we worked out these three types of business owners, and try to understand which one our clients are and then match them with a VA that can handle their personality.

Like a creator, we need to have an 'ideas parking spot'. We need to park all our ideas until our team is ready to implement them. We also need to make sure that we don't park ideas for too long, because the business needs to innovate and keep growing. We need to take one idea at a time and implement it, because that will help the business stay afloat.

It is essential that we find a balance between all three personality types. And I love to hang out with all the different personality types. I like to learn and suck up information from them. It helps me to develop the areas that I'm not as good at.

Even if I have developed some areas, it still drains me. And I don't think it's ever going to stop draining me to do those things that are not natural to me. But it's getting better, and I can do more. Now, when I plan my days, I always try to put in a whole day of business savvy. So I've got a day with numbers, meetings, and the like. I've got a day with content, where I do all the content stuff, and I've got a day of leading, where I would focus more on leading the team.

No matter which type of business owner you are, the key to success lies in recognising your strengths and weaknesses. By understanding where you excel and where you need support, you can build a team and a business strategy that leverages your natural abilities while addressing your challenges. Remember, it's not about fitting perfectly into one category, but rather about creating a balance that allows you to thrive as an entrepreneur. Whether you are a Creator, a Leader, or Business Savvy, embracing your unique traits and learning to work with others who complement your skills will lead to a more successful and fulfilling business journey.

Check out what type of business owner you are. Scan the code below:

WHAT TYPE OF BUSINESS OWNER ARE YOU?

An assessment form that determines your type of business owner.

SCAN THE CODE TO KNOW MORE

How do you find a Virtual Assistant?

Now that you understand your personality and what you're looking for, it's crucial to find a VA that matches your style. It's not just about skills–if you don't get along and can't work well together, hiring a VA won't be a positive experience and could end up being more time-consuming than necessary.

You have two main options to hire a Virtual Assistant: directly or through an agency. Finding and hiring a VA directly can be challenging and time-consuming. While some people use platforms like Upwork and OnlineJobs.ph, direct hiring requires patience as it might take three to four weeks dedicated to interviewing and screening of candidates.

Many Virtual Assistant agencies are available, which might seem overwhelming. The best approach is to ask your network, *"Have you got a VA? Where did you find them?"* Opt for an agency that comes recommended for a pleasant experience. Unfortunately, not all agencies create a beneficial environment for business owners, and you don't want to waste your time with those.

Direct hiring can be daunting and overwhelming with the vast online options. It's easy for people to take a job, say yes, and then fail to show up while still expecting to be paid. Many business owners randomly hire a virtual assistant for 10 or 20 hours a week for a project, not realising that the VA may not be fully utilising the time but still charging for it. This can foster an unhealthy relationship and momentum where VAs take advantage of employers, which isn't fair.

I'm not a huge fan of hiring directly. The primary benefit of going direct is lower costs, but then you lack supervision over your VA. If the VA leaves or becomes sick, you're left to manage alone, whereas an agency would typically provide a temporary replacement. When you hire directly, you also need to dedicate time to interview and screen applicants. Our agency, for instance, spends about 40 hours a week just on screening and interviewing candidates.

A great tip if you're hiring directly is to ask candidates to send a 90-second video. This approach screens candidates much faster because only about 10% of applicants will submit a video. It helps you avoid wasting time on those who aren't fully committed to even applying properly.

Another thing people often overlook is the cultural fit and determining if someone is just putting on a facade for the interview. People can perform exceptionally well in interviews but fail to follow through post-hire. We have specific questions we ask during our interviews to detect inconsistencies and ensure we're picking the right candidates.

It's not only about hiring a VA but also about retaining them. In our agency, we focus on our Virtual Assistants' wellness, mindset, and health. We provide a supportive network where they can collaborate, which adds incredible value and removes many worries about managing their well-being.

In today's environment, retaining staff long-term can be challenging. People often shop around, jumping from one job to another as agencies actively poach staff. We maintain a robust retention program to keep our Virtual Assistants happy and committed for the long haul, and we're fortunate that many stay with us because of the support and opportunities we provide.

Hiring a Virtual Assistant: Experience vs. Newcomers

We have one rule: hire based on attitude, not on experience. I firmly believe that experience doesn't matter if someone has the right attitude and is a fast learner. I want them in my team.

Having experience alone isn't everything! Without the right attitude, even the most experienced person can bring a negative vibe into the workspace. I prefer to work with people who have a positive outlook on life and are a great fit for the team.

Experience is irrelevant if they do not have the right attitude. A lot of times, and based on experience, experienced VAs who don't have a great attitude are so hard to train. They are set in their ways, they are not willing to change, they are not willing to learn something new, and it is quite hard and difficult to move them across and be faster. They are also easily employed because of their experience. And it is quite fascinating because, again, to me, it means nothing whether they have experience or not; what I want to see is their attitude, and what I want to see is how they work well on the job.

Obviously, we love to hire VAs with both outstanding attitudes and great experience on the job! We hire, train them, and provide experience within our agency, and as a result, we have a lot of VAs that have been with us for a while, and they are incredible.

Our Virtual Assistants have real-life office experience but are brand new to the VA world. They are open to learning. We teach them exactly how we want to work and how we want them to behave as a Virtual Assistant. We mould them the way that we believe works best to be a Virtual Assistant. And it has been a successful exercise.

We have over 70 clients now. That is because we have been able to train a Virtual Assistant from scratch to suit our clients' needs. They are loyal to us and you because they were given a chance. Filipinos are very loyal when they are given a chance. Often, they can have a can-do attitude, and we love that. They are willing to learn, willing to study, and willing to take extra courses, and that's what makes them exceptional in this field.

*Note to self: **Cultural Fit.** Hire people who fit your company's culture and share your values.*

Legal and Contractual Considerations and Security

Facing the challenges of international business can be daunting, particularly in the Philippines where local enforcement of international contracts may vary. This inconsistency can make some Virtual Assistants take these agreements less seriously. However, partnering with a reputable agency like ours can provide significant protection and assurance of compliance. Our clients trust us because we have implemented robust systems to safeguard their data and ensure that all contractual obligations are respected and adhered to.

Before introducing you to the operational platforms that will aid in managing your business, we ensure that all your passwords are securely stored in a central location such as *1Password* or *LastPass*. Often, businesses lose precious time retrieving forgotten passwords, which is not only frustrating but also inefficient. We establish secure systems complete with antivirus and computer security measures to ensure that your sensitive information is thoroughly protected, allowing you to access your passwords safely from anywhere.

Software/Platforms for Communication and Task Management
We openly share every platform, procedure, and resource with our clients. For instance, *Airtable* has proven invaluable for managing social media schedules, maintaining client databases, generating reports, and more. This collaborative approach ensures that our clients are equipped with the best tools and practices to enhance their operational effectiveness.

While *Airtable* is excellent for certain tasks, it does not replace project management tools like *Asana* or *Trello*, which are essential for helping Virtual Assistants stay on track with their assignments. For internal communications, we recommend *Slack* over platforms like WhatsApp, Messenger, or emails, as *Slack* offers a more structured and professional environment for team interactions.

Track the Virtual Assistant's time and productivity
For monitoring productivity and managing time effectively, we use tools like *Deputy* or *Time Doctor*. We suggest incorporating these into your operations as well, allowing you to check when your Virtual Assistant is online and facilitate payroll by providing a reliable reference for work hours logged. If you choose to work with our agency, we handle these aspects for you, ensuring each Virtual Assistant is compensated accurately and on time.

Security considerations when sharing access and information.
For sharing sensitive information, we recommend using services like *Dropbox* or *Google Drive* and providing Virtual Assistants with their own logins. This setup not only enhances security but also allows

for tracking and recovery of documents through version histories, adding an extra layer of accountability.

In preparation for integrating a Virtual Assistant into your business, it's beneficial to set up and familiarise yourself with these recommended platforms. This proactive approach will smooth the transition and enable you to leverage the full potential of your new team member effectively.

Note to self: Use Technology. *Leverage technology and software to automate processes wherever possible.*

Key Takeaways

- Finding a Virtual Assistant from platforms can be challenging, requiring careful effort to ensure reliability.
- Alternatively, engaging a reputable agency or using personal networks can make the search easier and more efficient.
- Direct hiring may cut costs, but lacks the supervision and quality assurance agencies provide.
- Cultural differences might affect communication and performance, but agencies are adept at managing these challenges.
- Prioritising attitude over experience ensures candidates are motivated to learn and grow in the role.
- Agencies offer detailed training and ongoing support, which fosters loyalty and dedication among Virtual Assistant s.
- Secure platforms like *1Password* or *LastPass* should be used for password management to maintain security.
- Tools such as *Airtable*, *Asana*, *Trello*, *Slack*, *Deputy*, and *Time Doctor* are key for task management and productivity tracking.

- Setting up these essential tools prepares you for a successful partnership with your Virtual Assistant.
- Hire based on attitude and not experience. It's a plus if they have a good attitude and experience.
- Realise where and what you are in the Business Owner type.

What actions are you going to take from this chapter?

1 _____

_____

_____

_____

_____

2 _____

_____

_____

_____

3 _____

_____

_____

_____

CHAPTER 5

EFFECTIVE ONBOARDING AND TRAINING

∞

When starting work with a Virtual Assistant, it's important that we are clear about what their role is going to be like, their job description, our expectations, the tasks that we want to pass along, what tasks are urgent and what are recurring. We want to make sure that they know what their role will be like. Clarity is power.

Passing along this clarity will help avoid any overwhelm for the Virtual Assistant.

Brainstorming Task
We mentioned the Brainstorm of tasks in chapter 3. It's a vital document that helps you map out the tasks your business needs you to delegate.

Why do I say your business and not you? See, when it's our own business, we are often attached to the outcome. We treat the business

as if it was our baby and sometimes with that energy, we don't make the right decisions for the business. My mentor once said: *"Francesca, all the decisions you make as a CEO are all for the business. What does the business need?"* Ask yourself: *"Does the business need me as the CEO to accomplish this task or will the business save time if we hire someone to take care of this role?"*

Note to self: Time and Energy Multiplication. *By delegating, you multiply your productivity and free up time to focus on high-level, strategic work that drives growth.*

Once we get clear on what the business needs, then we need to be realistic with the expectation of what a Virtual Assistant can do or what any human can actually accomplish in eight hours a day. Because sometimes, as business owners, we have the impression that we can do *a lot of things in eight hours.*

Now that the VA is about to start, we need to show them the brainstorm of tasks and identify which are the most important tasks we need to delegate and share how to do them.

We categorise the tasks in three phases. This way the VA can focus on learning all the tasks of phase one in their first month. This will avoid overwhelm and help the VA take ownership of those tasks so they can really be taken off your shoulders.

Many business owners try to rush this process, and say: *"Welcome to the team, here are the 40 hours' worth of tasks…"* Do intense training for two weeks and throw the VA in the deep end. I have noticed that this approach rarely works. I did it myself. By throwing my team in the deep end, they got used to reacting to the tasks I trained them to work on last minute things and not be proactive in the business. It was a recipe for disaster. Slow down to go faster became my MOTTO… I was resistant to it at the beginning because I LOVE everything fast, but then I realised I was doing a disservice not only to my team but also to my business.

When a VA starts with you, it's important that you do a handover meeting with all the team members that are going to be involved in the training of Phase 1 and your IT support to help them get set up with all the logins and platforms they need access to. Before the handover meeting, ensure you do a Team Meeting where you introduce the VA to the team. This will support the culture and help you avoid any disrespect within a team. When we help the team create a relationship amongst themselves, they are more likely to support one another rather than compete with one another.

Note to self: Calculate Your Buyback Rate. Determine how much your time is worth by calculating your hourly rate.

Handover Meeting

The handover meeting is a two-hour meeting on the VA's first day where you ensure your team helps the VA setup all the necessary platforms they will need to succeed at their job. I have seen it so many times, people firing a VA because they did not do certain jobs properly, because the VA had no access to all the platforms they needed to do the task properly. That is not fair, and we need to remember these people are not in the office with us. We need to help them get everything setup and running from the start.

As an agency, we arrange the handover meeting run by the supervisor we assign to the VA, so our clients have an experienced person guide them through this process. In this meeting, we set up all the required platforms to ensure the Virtual Assistant succeeds in their position. This is covered in our Setup for Success Course (our clients can access this as part of our setup process). In this course, we included platform and tools like *1Password*, *Slack*, *Airtable*—everything needed for a smoother relationship with a VA.

Setup Email for VA

We recommend that our clients set up an email address for their Virtual Assistants so that they can have a business calendar, and a business email, and they can feel that they are part of the business and feel that they're included by having their own login. I have seen many businesses run their company on a @gmail.com account.

I highly recommend your business email is @yourbusiness.com. Having a business email will make you look more professional and more credible to your clients.

Once you have helped the VA setup, we recommend you sit and look at the bigger picture of the business.

Overview of the Business

- What do you do?

- Who is your target market?

Even if someone is working in admin, we still want them to understand who your clients are and who you are dealing with, along with the important information they need to keep in mind.

If your business is an Immigration Agency, for example, you need to explain to the VA that your target market are people who are trying to move from one country to another. For an immigration agent, the VA work on their visa application is vital and this type of business would rely on NOT making mistakes in the documents. As an immigration agency you would highlight to the VA that they must triple check every document because it's going to be imperative in their migration. This view of the business helps the VA to understand the priorities and the most important thing that a Virtual Assistant needs to pay attention to.

What is the most important thing that your VA needs to pay attention to?

The Need for SOP and SOC

SOP stands for Standard Operating Procedures. Usually, businesses either don't have any procedures in place or if they do, they are outdated. One of the most important tasks I recommend business owners delegate is the creation of SOP. It's vital for the business and it will save a lot of pain if someone quits.

I used to get my team working on SOP for two weeks. Make them all updated and pretty and perfect and then forget to check it and forget to ensure my team kept them updated. Then suddenly one team member would leave and that's when I would realise my SOP was NOT updated... I wanted to cry!

So now, one of my rules in business is that my team MUST update SOPs weekly, and my managers need to check once a month randomly. When I didn't have managers in the team, I needed to be the one checking them.

If you have updated your SOPs but don't have SOCs (standard operating checklists), You must ensure your VA creates those checklists. As the VA is studying the SOPs, they can also develop the SOCs simultaneously. We will then collaborate to upload all the materials–templates, SOPs, and SOCs (which are checklists)– into *Asana* or *Trello* or simply on a google doc (my preferred option). Make sure that everything you've worked on is properly organised, accessible, and easy to follow.

If you don't have SOP, don't panic, you can take advantage of this new VA onboarding process and as you and your team teach the VA, ensure you record it on *Zoom*, the VA will watch it back and create SOP as they watch the recording. (We call this the Delegation Fast-Track Protocol).

I have learned a new way to do procedures I love and it has been so helpful to my team to understand it and stay on top of it, it's called 'Front End and Back End Procedures'.

Many businesses and corporations have procedure manuals that are long and detailed but still never explain the bigger picture. They never explain why you need to do these steps… and this missing part is the reason why employees cut corners. It's normal human behaviour. If we don't know why, we don't give it value, which means it's easy to drop. The Front End procedure is the procedure from the client perspective. It helps understand the end result of this task so that our employees pay attention to every fine detail. It's pretty powerful, and it's actually easier for a business owner's brain to write the Front End so that the team can write the Back End procedure. The Back End is simply this: all the steps the team needs to do behind the scenes for the client to receive the steps in the Front End Procedure.

Front End Procedure

It's crucial to map the Front End procedure from the perspective of the client or prospective client, focusing on outcomes, not just your tasks or your team's tasks. I recommend starting with the most common product or service that you sell. List down all your products and services in a Google doc and then select the most profitable one.

In my case, I would list all the services we offer, such as the Virtual Assistant Full-Time Package, Time Management Course, The Power of Delegation Book, etc.

I would then choose the Full-Time Virtual Assistant Package. The biggest challenge now is to keep reminding ourselves that we are writing the procedure from the client's perspective.

We ask ourselves:
What is the first thing that happens when people are potentially becoming a client?

They will find a landing page and learn about Empowering Virtual Solution from social media posts, and they want to book a call. So, they enquire to book a call and they will be sent a link.

Here's what it would look like:

- Client gets sent a link to book a call.
- The client will receive a calendar invite for the call via email.
- The client will receive a reminder to jump on the call.
- The client jumps on a call on *Zoom*.
- The client gets shown the procedures of our service.
- The client receives an agreement and signs it.
- The client pays via a link.
- The client receives a welcome email.

I love this process because now I can clearly see on one page what the clients go through when they are enquiring and signing up, and I can easily locate the gaps, improve our approach, and provide a better client experience.

Back End Procedure

Now, our team needs to go through each line of the Front End procedure and ensure they list all the steps they must take to ensure the client receives what is promised in the Front End Procedure. For example, for the client to be able to book a call, what does my team at the back end of the business need to do to make sure that these steps happen effortlessly?

Every day at the beginning of each shift, a VA will need to ensure that the landing page is working and there is enough time available in the sales team's calendar for the client to book a call. If there isn't enough time, they will reach out to the sales team to update their calendar. Once the client books a call, we have an automated message in *Slack* that lets us know a client has booked a call. Then there is another form that collects what the potential clients have filled out. One of the VAs will take the form, copy it, and input it into our CRM.

Once that's done, everything will be in the back end. I helped a client create their Front End procedure from scratch, and they were like, *"Oh my goodness, why did I not know this strategy before?"* It's priceless. You will have all the Front End, all the Back End done and one more thing that we add at the top of the Front End is product information. It's like, what does this product include, and how much is it?

These are our SOPs (Standard Operating Procedures); we call them Front End and Back End, and we document them in writing on our Google Doc. We don't necessarily create *Zoom* videos for these; we prefer to keep it simple with just screenshots.

If there is something more complicated and visual, then yes, we will do a video and also include the link for someone to watch. This allows us to cater to all types of learners. However, I am not a big fan of video tutorials because they can become outdated very easily, and then we have to record them again. I prefer screenshots because it's easy for my team to update a screenshot. If you choose a video format and the platform you mentioned in the video changes, you will have to record all the videos again.

Tools and Technologies to Facilitate Communication and Task Management

Take your VA through the basics of your CRM or Task management system to ensure they know how to navigate it. Most VAs would have learned use one of these platforms, and usually, once you know how to use one, the rest are pretty self-explanatory and VAs can typically work out how to use them quickly.

Overview of the Role and the Expectations, and Business Rules

It's important to go through this so that the VA understands what their position in the business is and who they must report to.

I would like to explain what is urgent for us in this business and what the expected response times are for VAs when they are tagged on slack or emailed by you or other team members. Sometimes we take these unspoken rules for granted, but they can truly help your VA succeed if we explain them clearly from the beginning.

I have gone to the extent of creating a Business RULES file, where I share all the rules of the business. This file summarises and reminds my team of my expectations. I am going to share this here for you to reference and create one for yourself.

COMPANY RULES

VALUES:

1. We respect each other no matter what.
2. We are all about leveling up.
3. We got your back.
4. We are committed to your success.

GOOGLE DRIVE:

- NEVER save a document on your own computer. Always save it on *Google Drive* – ALWAYS. This will prevent any file from being lost.

CALENDAR:

- NEVER EVER EVER reschedule a meeting.
- NEVER EVER be late for a meeting.
- Use your calendar for everything.
- Have an IDEAL week and keep updating it every six months.
- Always accept meetings for the following month on the first day of the month.
- On Friday afternoon, work on the next week's calendar and plan the week.

EMAIL:

- Use an email signature.
- When on LEAVE always set an out-of-office reply in your emails and on your phone.
- Keep your INBOX 0 every DAY!
- Only keep in your inbox emails that you are still working on.
- File away emails into folders.
- Answer all emails within two working hours.

PHONE:
- Update your Voicemail.
- Respond to ALL SMS within 4 hours (during working hours).
- Listen to ALL voicemails daily.
- Open ALL messages and calls so the phone shows 0 unread.

Slack:
- Keep notifications on, EXCEPT when you are in meetings.
- Check *Slack* in between meetings.
- Have the word URGENT set up as a notification, no matter your status.
- Always reply in THREADS (even in personal channels).

1Password
- Every team member must use *1Password* when searching for a login.
- DO NOT search for a platform on Google.
- Search via the *1Password* extension.
- Send your secret key to Bebs (for Bebs to save under Management folder)
- Do not save any passwords in your private vaults (all passwords must be saved in the common vault you have been added to)
- Save ALL your logins in *1Password*.

NEVER save passwords on the computer, Chrome, or Safari.
- Switch off the save passwords feature on Chrome or Safari.

ZOOM settings:

- Go into the *Zoom* settings and ensure ALL recordings are saved in ZOOM TO MOVE (and then our team will move them to the correct VIDEO folder).
- ALWAYS record to the cloud (not on the computer).

COMPUTER SETUP:

- Download *Slack* as an app on the computer and phone.
- Download *1Password* as an app on computer and phone and as extension in Chrome.
- Use keywords to set up shortcuts to save time (System Settings + Keyboard + Text Replacement).

ATTENTION TO DETAILS

- Always have 2 people triple-checking your work (emails, SMS, messages, LPs, buttons).

TASK ASSIGNATION

It will be very useful to go through the brainstorm of tasks file with your VA and say: *"This is your role and expectation; these are the things you are going to focus on together with our team in Phases 1, 2, and 3."*

THE THREE ONBOARDING PHASES

Phase one

Before the VA starts, we must determine the initial tasks to delegate and hold the VA responsible for.

When I choose Phase One, I try not to focus on what is urgent but rather on the most important and simpler tasks I can pass along so the VA can ease into the role.

This also gives you the chance to understand if you can work well together. Some people spend too much time in training in the first month and not enough doing, which means they think the VA is learning and has grasped it all, and they don't get a chance to see the VA in the actual job until month two… which often is too late to make the tough decision to let them go if they don't perform.

I prefer to teach one task fully and let them do it, and I will check it, until I am sure they have got it. Then we move on to the second task. This allows me to determine if me and the VA are on the same page.

We need to keep in mind that we should always hire slowly and fire fast. There is no point in dragging someone along if we can already tell from the beginning that it is not working out.

Our goal is to ensure compatibility between both parties. It's become clear on several occasions that the Virtual Assistant may not be the ideal choice for a client, leading us to question if we should assign them to someone else. We're not sure. And then we match the VA with someone who has a completely different energy, vibe, direction, and leadership, and this Virtual Assistant shines working alongside them. Remember, it's not about the VA's capability, it's about finding the right match for you and your needs.

We need to remember that when we fire fast, it is not because we're neglecting them and not taking care of them. We're firing fast because we don't want them to stay working with someone who is not a good match for them. We can find a better client for them. So, once we have decided which one is Phase One, Phase Two, and Phase Three, we literally put all those things in a column, so we know exactly what we're going to focus on for the first month. This also helps us manage our own expectations because, I don't know about you, but I work very fast. If I am working with someone and don't follow the plan, I might think, *"Oh, my goodness, it's been a month, and this person has accomplished nothing yet." But what was the priority? What did you say you wanted the VA to achieve in their first month? Then realise, "Oh, the VA has completed all of Phase One."*

Clarity is power, and this 3-Phase method has saved a lot of time and money for our clients. I highly recommend you follow it too.

Phase Two
Phase Two usually coincides with month two. Sometimes the VA picks up things faster, and you can move to phase 2 earlier, but I would NOT move to this phase until I am confident that the VA is already independently working on all the tasks from Phase One. There is no rush to move to Phase Two. The VA will become faster at picking up tasks. Try not to rush Phase One, which is the harder phase, as the VA needs to learn everything about your business here. You will be surprised how quickly they will learn Phases Two and Three. So take your time, and remember–slow down to go faster.

Phase Three
This final Phase is where I like to give my VA a little more responsibility and a little more independence. I choose more complicated tasks for this phase. By now, the VA should have clarity on our business and will handle tasks like applying for grants and awards, answering emails, etc.

Note to self: Limitations of DIY Thinking. *Trying to do everything yourself restricts what you can accomplish.*

TRAINING YOUR VA FOLLOWING THE DELEGATION FAST TRACK PROTOCOL

1. Start with One Task from Phase One – It's crucial to grasp the concept of training. Tasks that recur weekly need to be transitioned off your plate–but not immediately stopped, as you'll initially do them alongside your VA. You might perform the task with the VA observing, or vice versa. This initial stage involves some micromanagement, as it's all about showing the VA how things are done in your business.

    Choose a key recurring task and collaborate on it. For instance, conduct a *Zoom* call where you share your screen, perform every step of the task, and have the session recorded. This helps in understanding why each step is necessary and the frequency and implications of these tasks. The goal here is to ensure everything is captured correctly so the VA can take over effectively.

2. Follow the Delegation Fast-Track Protocol. Here's a brief rundown: the goal during your training *Zoom* calls is for the VA to record the session and draft an SOP (Standard Operating Procedure) from it. Your role is to review and refine the SOP to ensure accuracy. This may require several iterations to perfect. Once finalised, you'll have a reliable SOP that ensures the task is completed correctly going forward.

3. Supervise, Don't Micromanage – Learning to supervise without micromanaging is key. Initially, consider daily brief meetings to review progress. This phase involves repeatedly applying the Delegation Fast Track Protocol until the VA can independently handle the tasks. Such regular check-ins

help transition responsibilities smoothly without the need for constant overseeing.

4. After a few weeks of closely working with your VA, you'll begin to see their capabilities, which is crucial for effectively planning their week. This understanding also helps shape your own ideal week. We offer training on this to all our clients as part of our time management course, which has proven beneficial for many business owners. The course is designed to help even those who are already highly organised to further fine-tune their schedules. If you're interested, you can scan a code at the end of this book for a significant discount on this course, which has garnered excellent reviews for its effectiveness in boosting organisational skills.

What we aim to do is assign all tasks to your VA, and this should be scheduled on an *Airtable* base. Once you're happy with the setup for the first week, from Monday to Friday, and for subsequent weeks, you'll then be able to create recurring events in your calendar. This ensures that every Monday you're working on the back end of the business, or perhaps every Monday afternoon you dedicate time for client interactions.

Approval process on *Dropbox* or *Google Drive*

By setting up systems for accountability and feedback, we've implemented something called the Approval Process within our *Dropbox* or *Google Drive* or whichever digital storage you prefer. Here's how it works: We create project folders, and each folder is categorised by department. Each department is tasked with a project, and within those, folders are organised by the team member responsible for the approval system. For instance:

- The initial check is assigned to Team Member 1, marked as 1. (TM 1 Name).
- After their review, it moves to Team Member 2, noted as 2. (TM 2 Name).
- Finally, the last review before approval comes to me, noted as 3. FM to Approve. Subsequent folders include 4. FM Approved for items I've approved.
- To Edit for outputs needing edits.
- Not Approved for items needing rework.

For example, in a Marketing Project:
1. VA to check
2. CEO to Approve
3. CEO Approved
4. Team to Edit
5. CEO Not Approved

1. Schedule a meeting with your VA to give feedback
Every week, I set aside time in my calendar for editing and approving items. Once I approve something, I move it into the appropriate folder. If it needs editing, it goes into the 'To Edit' folder, and if another team member's approval is needed, it's moved to the 'To Approve' folder. We ensure everyone on the team has scheduled times to review and approve work, ensuring tasks continuously progress.

2. How to Give Feedback
Initially, it's crucial to review tasks together with your VA to teach them and improve their understanding of unapproved work, helping them to enhance their performance. When providing feedback:

- Be kind and compassionate with your Virtual Assistant.
- Explain why certain things need to be done your way. (there is always a reason behind our systems, and if we don't explain it, they won't be able to remember it).
- Help them create templates and quick replies and FAQs, so that they don't have to think much and can just follow the process. That's what I love to do. Behind everything, there is a process, there's a procedure, and there is a system. We need to extract that idea from our minds and enlist the VA's assistance to develop and execute it.

It's essential not only to start well but to maintain the momentum. Continual training and upskilling your VA are crucial for retaining them long-term and keeping them motivated. Involve them actively in the work processes so they can progress to roles they are passionate about. People excel when they love what they do. To support their development, offer monthly training tailored to industry updates and organise an annual retreat for team building and skill enhancement. This ongoing educational commitment ensures your team remains up-to-date and effective in their roles.

Key Takeaways

- Define job descriptions, tasks, expectations, and priorities when starting with a Virtual Assistant (VA).
- Preparation ensures alignment and prevents misunderstandings.
- Before hiring, map out tasks and create a realistic workload plan, considering the time required for each task.
- Phase the onboarding process by starting with simple tasks to evaluate the match between you and the VA.

- Use tools like *Airtable*, *Asana*, and *Slack* for efficient communication and task management.
- Provide structured training and create Standard Operating Procedures (SOPs) to guide the VA.
- Implement systems for accountability and regular feedback.
- Foster a supportive environment by being kind and compassionate.
- Make sure to establish protocols or procedures like Approval system or Company rules so you and VA are both on the same page
- Continual training and upskilling your VA are crucial for retaining them long-term and keeping them motivated

What actions are you going to take from this chapter?

1 _____

_____

_____

_____

_____

2 _____

_____

_____

_____

_____

3 _____

_____

_____

_____

_____

CHAPTER 6

TIME MANAGEMENT MASTERY WITH YOUR VIRTUAL ASSISTANT

∞

Time management is crucial in our business, especially when coordinating with a Virtual Assistant (VA). Effective scheduling ensures that *Zoom* meetings occur as planned. Disorganisation can lead to a lack of interaction with the VA, potentially causing disconnection and ultimately the loss of valuable assistance. As someone naturally bursting with ideas, I've had to learn to structure my time meticulously to prevent my creativity from disrupting our schedules–though I'll admit, I still throw a curveball into our plans now and then (haha!).

Benefits of Time Management

Just the other day, I was discussing time management with a friend who employs 30 people. He mentioned feeling like his team was disorganised and not adhering to their daily schedules. After they began my time management course as a group, he noticed a significant improvement in productivity.

Often, productivity is mistakenly associated with working overtime to complete daily tasks, but I disagree with this approach. I advocate for working fewer hours–say six instead of eight–ensuring those hours are intensely productive, with no procrastination. It's a common observation: the more time we think we have, the more time we take.

Proper time management reduces stress by allowing us to prioritise and enjoy activities, rather than constantly reacting to work demands. Improved time management leads to business growth. Having more time for money making activities and feeling accomplished leads to a better lifestyle.

Working on priority, understanding how important it is to strategically prioritise some tasks over others enhances this approach. Recognising the tasks that require immediate attention and those that can be scheduled for later is key to effective time management, ensuring that each day is not only productive but also balanced.

Note to self: Invest Time Wisely. Reinvest your newly freed time into activities that grow your business.

Strategies for Prioritising Tasks

1. Focus on Money-Making Activities First: The primary focus of any business should be on activities that generate revenue. Every task that contributes directly to business growth should be prioritised to ensure sustained operations and profitability.

2. Retention of Clients, Products or Services: These are crucial elements around which the business operations should revolve. Every team member must continually evaluate their daily contributions to these key areas: generating revenue and retaining clients. These are vital because, without them, the sustainability of every position within the company would be at risk.

Reacting to the business and staying occupied with tasks that are not impactful will not only be inefficient but also lead to burnout. It may create an illusion of busyness, yet with little to no focus on the tasks that truly matter.

Ditch the List

In my time management course, I advocate moving away from maintaining a perpetual digital task list. These lists are often filled with 'wishful' tasks that most people never get around to completing. Because they end up constantly reacting to immediate business needs, which derails their planned tasks. Recognising the difference between what's urgent, what's important, what's not important, and what should not be a priority is critical.

To minimise tasks that suddenly become urgent and to work more effectively on proactive business growth, it's advisable to abandon the traditional to-do list. When individuals work from a list, they tend to pick tasks they enjoy, which may not align with business priorities and can take up disproportionate amounts of time. Furthermore, interruptions typical in a business environment can lead to a continuous cycle of reactivity. This often results in unfinished tasks and growing anxiety over what hasn't been accomplished.

Ideal Week Setup for You and Your VA
We have created a strategy called the Ideal Week:

1. **Make a list of all the tasks.** Begin by jotting down everything you handle–daily, weekly, monthly, quarterly, and yearly. This inventory is crucial as it prompts you to reconsider whether you want to continue these tasks or delegate them. After cataloguing these tasks, you'll likely discover additional free time. For instance, when I was optimising my VA's schedule, I organised tasks into columns by frequency and then grouped them by type. For client communications–whether with current, past or potential clients–I categorised these under a specific label

like Client Communication. This systematic categorisation streamlines task management and enhances the efficiency of prioritisation.

2. **Map out your week.** Integrate these tasks into your weekly schedule. For example, if client communication is your forte, and you prefer handling these in the morning, schedule them accordingly. Understanding and aligning with your personal work preferences is crucial. This structure prevents you from merely reacting to business demands. By setting specific times for client interactions and back-end tasks like meetings and projects, you gain control over your schedule. Break down these responsibilities, assign them on your calendar, and visualise your ideal week–this ensures a balanced approach to both client engagement and business management.

3. **Align with your strengths.** Focus on what you excel at and enjoy doing. Avoid setting unrealistic expectations that might lead to stress or a sense of failure. Incorporate breaks, like time for coffee or checking emails, into your schedule. This detailed planning aids in crafting a successful week, allowing you to work more efficiently on the business rather than getting bogged down in day-to-day operations.

4. **Proactive Self Compassion.** The most significant barrier to maintaining this schedule is often our own mindset. For instance, when the calendar signals it's time to record a podcast or write a chapter, my mind might start racing with all the other tasks I need to tackle, tempting me to procrastinate. This is why I hold frequent meetings with my team–to keep myself accountable. Having a larger team

allows for regular check-ins without overburdening any single member. If you have a smaller team, it's crucial to balance time spent in meetings with allowing team members sufficient time to complete their tasks independently.

Note to self: Clear Expectations. Provide clear instructions, expectations and outcomes for delegated tasks.

Follow the Calendar

1. **Avoid procrastination.** Now, the main challenge is our brain. It will try to procrastinate, to resist, to sabotage your schedule. You must treat your calendar as your boss. Remember, you set your schedule because you are your own boss, but you must adhere to it strictly. Each day, focus on how to stick to the calendar. How can you ensure that everything planned is accomplished? Once you manage this, you've mastered your ideal week. Next, apply the same discipline with your VA, and review weekly to assess if you stuck to the plan.

2. **Your Calendar is your boss.** I treat my calendar seriously. For instance, today it was scheduled for an EVS one-hour slot to record this book, covering chapters six and seven. Even when my brain nudges me towards procrastination, my VA ensures I remain on track, reminding me, *"We need to complete this by June 3rd, let's get it done!"* This helps me stay on schedule and finish tasks as planned.

In practice, if you have a task following a meeting, immediately schedule it in your next available slot in the calendar and include task details in the meeting notes. This is more effective than jotting it down on a random piece of paper. This method reinforces trust in your scheduling; what's in your calendar will get done. No excuses, no rescheduling–just execute it. This approach has proven successful with my team as well.

I've designed an ideal week for myself where all tasks and meetings requiring my attention are meticulously scheduled. I work a maximum of 24 hours a week; these hours are intense and well-organised, allowing me the rest of the week to enjoy life!

If you're interested in creating a similarly structured week, you can learn more about it in my Time Management course, available at the end of this book.

Note to self: *Your calendar is your boss.*

Key Takeaways

- Mastering time management is crucial for CEOs to lead and teach Virtual Assistants (VAs) effectively.
- Organising and structuring time boosts productivity, reduces stress, and allows more focus on money-making activities, leading to business growth and a better lifestyle.
- Prioritising essential tasks like money-making and client retention prevents burnout from busy work.
- Avoid relying solely on digital lists, which can result in unfinished tasks and reactive work patterns.
- Understand task urgency and importance for better decision-making.
- Create an 'ideal week' schedule for yourself and your VA, mapping out tasks in a calendar.
- Work according to your strengths, including breaks and manageable tasks.
- Treat your calendar like your boss, stick to it, and ensure all tasks are completed.
- Regularly review and adjust your schedule to stay on track.
- Teach these time management strategies to your VAs for a cohesive team approach.
- This method boosts productivity and ensures your team focuses on the business's top priorities.

What actions are you going
to take from this chapter?

1 _____

_____

_____

_____

_____

2 _____

_____

_____

_____

3 _____

_____

_____

_____

CHAPTER 7

RETAIN YOUR VIRTUAL ASSISTANT – BUILDING A CULTURE FOR LONG TERM SUCCESS

∞

Building a strong relationship with your Virtual Assistant and cultivating a supportive company culture are crucial for retaining team members long-term.

Create Long Term Commitment

There's no shortage of demand for Virtual Assistants, with plenty of competition and opportunities for them to move from one business to another. It's becoming increasingly challenging to foster commitment and retain personnel over the long haul–but it's certainly not impossible. We aim to keep those who are a good fit for our business, those who are eager to grow and develop with us and are truly committed to the business's growth. We don't keep people merely for convenience; we want team members who are genuinely aligned with our goals.

Working Harmoniously

The right workplace culture is essential. Without it, it's difficult to discern whether team members are a good fit. Once you start implementing the correct cultural elements, it becomes apparent when someone doesn't mesh well with the team. You might find yourself wondering why you kept someone who was never the right fit from the start. This often happens because the right structures weren't in place to identify misalignments early on.

So, what constitutes the right culture? It begins with clarity on your business values. Before hiring, make sure that these values are well-defined and understood. Hire individuals who share these values to ensure a good match. The right culture doesn't just happen; it's consciously built, one interaction and one individual at a time. It's about mutual respect and embedding this ethos in everything you do within the company.

Be clear about the type of environment you want in your business and make decisions that align with this vision. This proactive approach ensures you create a workplace where everyone feels valued and communication is clear, fostering a productive and positive environment.

For the Business to Succeed

We aim to establish a long-term commitment because hiring the right people allows them to advance and excel within the business, which benefits everyone involved. When the work is enjoyable, everything else flows smoothly. I often say, *"If it's not fun, it's not worth it."* Hard work is essential because without it, there won't be time for leisure. Without the right team, you'll constantly be drawn back into day-to-day business operations.

For the Clients to Feel Love

Taking good care of your team ensures they, in turn, take care of your clients. As CEOs, our primary job is to nurture our team—that's fundamentally what we need to focus on.

For the VA to Feel Involved and Cared for

"Take care of your team and they'll take care of your clients."
When VAs feel valued and cared for, they invest themselves in your business and your clients. This principle is a cornerstone of creating a workplace where no one–clients or VAs–wants to leave.

Best practices for communicating with your VA

Without a strong relationship, a Virtual Assistant might feel disconnected, which can lead to them quitting or underperforming, making the workplace a challenging environment for everyone. So, how do we cultivate a healthy, productive relationship?

1. **Create a strong relationship.** Start by establishing clear expectations. It's crucial to communicate openly from the beginning about what behaviours you expect and what you won't tolerate. I value honesty above all; it's better to face the hard truths together than to avoid them.

2. **Your Virtual Assistant is not a slave.** They are not just workers; they are integral to your business. Treating them with the same respect and professionalism you would offer a valued client helps cultivate a healthy working environment. Since I started to treat my team like I treat my clients, the whole environment has changed. I had to ask myself... *"Would I treat or speak to a client like this? NOPE... so why do I treat my most valuable asset like this?"*

3. **Don't avoid or ignore them.** What if we build a relationship with a Virtual Assistant as if they were our client? We wouldn't avoid or ignore them. We'd address issues, communicate openly, and understand what's going right and what isn't. Treat interactions with your VA as if they were client meetings. Don't just dismiss concerns or avoid discussions. A positive, open relationship helps resolve issues constructively.

4. **Be on time and make them feel important and respected.** Always be punctual for meetings. Making your VAs feel respected and important reduces stress and enhances productivity. It's crucial to show respect in every interaction, reinforcing that they are valued members of the team.

Note to self: Importance of Relationships. Success comes from relationships, not isolated effort.

Tools and Strategies to Enhance Collaboration.
I'll share with you some of these tools and strategies for enhancing collaboration with the Virtual Assistant. By implementing these strategies, you can create a more engaged and cooperative team environment, leading to higher productivity and better results for your business.

1. **Regular Meetings.** Regular team meetings are crucial. We conduct ours weekly, keeping them between 30 to 45 minutes–brief enough to remain focused yet substantial enough to cover important ground. This also allows time for personal breaks like checking emails or stepping away briefly.

2. **Daily huddle.** Start each day with a quick team huddle to discuss daily priorities and tasks. This not only clarifies focus areas but also fosters a sense of accountability. Encourage team members to ask questions and share their goals for the day. This interaction is particularly inspiring when conducted in a group setting, as it can motivate team members by exposing them to the work pace and dedication of their peers. Questions I ask during the huddles:

- What are your wins?
- What are you working on today?
- What are your priorities?
- Where do you focus?
- What do you want to achieve today?
- What is your biggest challenge right now?

This is nice to do in teams rather than one-on-one because, obviously, if you have more than one thing, one member can also listen to what other people aren't doing. And they can be inspired, like, *"Oh, wow, these people do so many things and only share one thing; maybe I should improve my way of doing it."* It's good to do it together.

3. **Lighten up communication.** Have fun, and don't be too serious. Use platforms like *Slack* not just for work-related discussions but also to inject some fun into the dialogue. A light-hearted conversation can significantly boost team morale.

4. **Personal Share.** Make an effort to share personal stories about your life—like updates about your family or recent trips—and encourage your team to do the same. This builds deeper connections and makes the work environment more personable and supportive.

5. **Value ALL ideas. Be interested in Virtual Assistant's ideas.** Emphasise that no idea is too small or silly; everybody and every idea is welcome. That is one rule I embody in my business. I make sure that all ideas from my team are addressed. That way, it will develop a sense of belongingness, and the VA will feel they are valued. Encourage your team

to speak up and share their thoughts, which helps to nurture an inclusive and innovative workplace atmosphere.

6. **Open Communication.** Ask for their opinion and keep the communication open. Trust your Virtual Assistant, and they will trust you. This is something that I've noticed in a lot of clients: they don't trust the Virtual Assistant; they micromanage them… I used to do the same. Always seek and value the opinions of your Virtual Assistants. Keeping communication channels open and trusting their input can lead to higher job satisfaction and loyalty.

7. **Trust your VA and they will trust you.** Trust your VAs to handle their responsibilities without micromanagement. However, if trust is breached, it's crucial to address the issue directly and work on rebuilding that trust, though it can be challenging to restore fully once damaged.

8. **Incentive Trips.** Promise an occasional trip to your country for your VAs to work from the office, coupled with a team retreat. This not only gives them a change of scenery but also serves as a significant bonding and team-building opportunity.

Note to self: *Foster Accountability: Hold your team accountable for results without micromanaging.*

What if you don't have time to nurture the relationship with the VA?

I say you cannot afford not to make time. The VA deserves your time, and together, you can become a force of nature. Your business will undoubtedly benefit from this investment. If you neglect this aspect, you'll likely regret it, as you may learn the hard way. Without proper attention, your VA might leave, forcing you to start the hiring and training process from scratch. It's vital and inevitable to build a nurturing culture so you can retain people long-term. Neglecting to do so means you'll continually see turnover. We have a VA who has been with us for seven years, and there's a clear reason for it: our culture is unbeatable.

Key Takeaways

- In a competitive market, building a strong relationship with your Virtual Assistant (VA) and fostering a supportive team culture is crucial.
- VAs have many options, making it essential to create an environment where they feel valued and committed.
- Focus on attracting and retaining individuals who align with your business goals and are eager to grow with it.
- A positive culture helps identify the right team members, boosting both productivity and client satisfaction.
- Regular communication, structured meetings, and using tools like *Slack* for fun and personal interactions strengthen team bonds.
- Trust is key–empower your VA with autonomy and respect their input to build a lasting partnership.
- Investing time in nurturing this relationship is vital for long-term success.
- This approach fosters loyalty and stability within your business, ensuring your team stays aligned and motivated.
- Right workplace culture is essential in making sure your VA stays with you.
- Take care of your VAs and they will take care of your clients and business.

What actions are you going to take from this chapter?

1 _____

_____

_____

_____

_____

2 _____

_____

_____

_____

_____

3 _____

_____

_____

_____

_____

CHAPTER 8

SOCIAL MEDIA DELEGATION PLAN

∞

Can you really delegate Social Media to a Virtual Assistant? Absolutely. Here's how I explain it: Think of Virtual Assistants as the drivers of a car. You, as the CEO, need to provide the car (which represents the social media tools) and the GPS (your goals and strategy for what you want to achieve on social media). Without a car and GPS, the VA will be wandering aimlessly without direction.

Things People Say to Me All the Time

- *"Oh, it doesn't take me too long to do social media. I can handle it myself."*
- *"I don't mind doing social media. I can keep that task going."*
- *"Nobody else can do social media like me. I want people to feel my presence, so I'm going to have to keep doing it."*

When I hear these, I always think, *"What? No, of course, there's a way to delegate."*

The Importance of Social Media in Today's Business Landscape

Social media is one task you definitely should not be doing yourself. It should be delegated, especially as a CEO, where your focus should be elsewhere. So, why is social media crucial for us business owners?

In 2024 and beyond, maintaining a social media presence is essential. We need to prioritise it.

- **Visibility and Verification**: people will find and vet us through social media. In today's digital age, it's crucial to be visible on these platforms and to stay abreast of digital marketing trends. Missing out on this means sticking to outdated methods, losing out on current news, and trends. Just recently, a client commented, *"Hold on, you only have*

10 Google reviews, but that's like having just 10 clients?" That really puts things into perspective, doesn't it?

- **Perceptions of Success**: when people don't see active social media or a strong number of reviews, they might view your business as unsuccessful. Many discover our services through Google and social media. If we're not present there, we miss out on those opportunities. If potential clients see nothing, they assume nothing significant is happening.
- **Making the Right Impression**: if potential clients find valuable and engaging content on your social media, it helps them decide to work with you. Conversely, a lack of engaging content might drive them to choose your competitor who has a more robust social media presence. That's just how it works!

Thus, being hands-off with social media isn't feasible, especially in the initial years of your business. I advise my clients to actively engage by recording videos–perhaps one a week–with a Virtual Assistant on *Zoom*. This content can be transcribed and repurposed into blogs, newsletters, and posts. This strategy is crucial as it increases exposure and helps your audience connect with you across various mediums.

Tasks to Delegate to your Social Media VA

- **Social Media Management**: oversee all social media accounts.
- **Social Media Scheduling/Posting**: ensure content is scheduled and posted timely.
- **Content Creation and Repurposing**: develop new content and repurpose existing content.

- **Video Editing:** enhance raw video footage for social media posts.
- **Transcription:** convert video or audio content into written format.
- *LinkedIn, TikTok, Instagram,* and *Facebook* **Strategies:** apply specific strategies tailored to each platform.
- **Lead Generation:** use social media to generate new business leads.

It's crucial for us to focus only on tasks that require our personal touch, such as creating a few key videos each month to keep our presence fresh and relevant. For instance, I have a friend who is a migration agent; she keeps a handful of clients to stay informed about new developments in her field. This approach is vital for her to remain updated on industry trends. Similarly, being the face of your business and updating your audience with quick video clips on platforms like TikTok can be very effective. These snippets can then be transcribed and adapted for different social media channels, maximising your visibility and engagement.

Note to self: Focus on Results, Not Methods. Allow your team to find their way to achieve the desired results.

Creating a Social Media Strategy and Calendar

Our approach to social media marketing emphasises the power of organic strategies, distinct from paid advertising methods. If you're looking to effectively engage on platforms like *Facebook* without the immediate need for ads, our Organic Facebook Marketing Course is invaluable. This course offers comprehensive insights into building an organic presence, which is crucial groundwork before venturing into paid advertising. Implementing organic strategies not only enhances your visibility but also strengthens your brand's authenticity and connection with your audience.

We recommend developing a robust social media strategy and calendar. Here's a summary of what our course covers:

1. **Using *Airtable*:** we utilise *Airtable* for planning our social media content instead of using it as a scheduler for posting because we've found that live engagement significantly boosts effectiveness. When our Virtual Assistants manage and post content directly to platforms like *Facebook*, *Instagram*, and *LinkedIn*, it enhances our presence. These platforms prioritise live, real-time content over scheduled posts because they seek active, engaged users. Using a scheduler might result in fewer views and interactions since these platforms favour content that attracts immediate attention. Although I'm not personally active on social media, I recognise the importance of engagement in driving sales. While you might opt to schedule posts over the weekend when you prefer not to work, it's crucial during the week to post live at times when your audience is most engaged. It's important to adjust this approach weekly, as setting and forgetting scheduled posts often fails to yield desired results. When clients ask about the benefits of their long-standing social media efforts, they're often disappointed. The key lies in active engagement—not just posting but also interacting with the audience. 'Live engagement' means your Virtual Assistant manually copies the post details and images from *Airtable* and posts them directly onto social media platforms, ensuring real-time interaction and presence.

2. **Social Media and Events Calendar – Planning in Advance:** planning in advance is crucial; remember, failing to plan is planning to fail. Many businesses often find themselves organising events at the last minute, which puts undue pressure on their team members. To avoid this, it's essential to stay organised and plan your events and corresponding social media strategies 6-12 months in advance. This advance planning allows your team to strategise effectively and prepare content that can be posted 4-6 weeks before the actual event, ensuring a well-prepared and less stressful execution. This approach not only eases the workload but also enhances the effectiveness of your promotions, giving your audience ample time to engage with the upcoming event information.

3. **Video Recording Strategy:** we utilise a proactive video recording strategy. My Virtual Assistants conduct research to identify the latest viral trends on platforms like TikTok and *Instagram* Reels. This research helps in planning the content that I can teach, particularly during sales or discovery calls with clients. After these calls, my VAs transcribe the discussions and extract topics that resonate with potential clients' challenges. This process provides invaluable insights that we use to create targeted video content addressing these specific business issues.

Once the content is ready, my VA and I collaborate to record the videos. This collaborative effort ensures that the content is not only informative but also engaging. After recording, these videos are strategically distributed across our social media platforms, ensuring maximum reach and impact. This approach not only enhances our social media presence but also provides real-time solutions to our audience, making our strategy both effective and invaluable.

Note to self: Free Yourself from Social Media. Automate or delegate social media tasks so you can focus on strategy.

Monitoring and Measuring Social Media Performance

Regular meetings with your Virtual Assistant are essential for effective monitoring and measurement of your social media performance. It's important to have scheduled weekly, monthly, and quarterly sessions to refine your strategy and ensure it aligns with your business goals.

- **Weekly Meetings:** Discuss ongoing strategies, review immediate results, and adjust tactics as needed. Use these meetings to get updates on ongoing projects and track key performance metrics closely.
- **Monthly Meetings:** review KPIs from the previous month, monitor social media growth through detailed reports from your VA, and conduct what we call a 'pulse meeting' to ensure we keep our finger on the pulse of our marketing performance.
- **Quarterly Reviews:** evaluate the broader impact of your social media efforts, including brand engagement and audience growth. Use these reviews to plan for future public holidays specials or marketing initiatives.
- **Annual Assessments:** set strategic goals for the coming year based on a detailed performance analysis, ensuring that your social media strategies are aligned with your business objectives.

- **Reviewing Reports:** your VA should provide comprehensive reports detailing key performance indicators (KPIs) such as viewer engagement, conversion rates, and overall social media interactions. These reports will track not only views but also how many people clicked on your posts, booked calls, made purchases, and other relevant actions.
- **Setting and Monitoring KPIs:** clearly establish and regularly review KPIs for your Virtual Assistants to gauge their success and identify areas needing improvement.
- **Accountability:** embrace the principle that 'Doers don't do what checkers don't check.' Regular checks on your social media systems and marketing efforts are essential to maintain consistency and drive effectiveness. By holding each other accountable, you ensure sustained effort and meticulous attention to detail in your social media campaigns.

Key Takeaways

- In today's business landscape, having a robust social media presence is essential for visibility and growth.
- Many business owners resist delegating social media tasks, thinking they can handle it themselves or that no one else can represent their brand properly.
- This mindset, however, can limit business potential and growth opportunities.
- To remain competitive and relevant, CEOs must embrace delegation by entrusting skilled Virtual Assistants to manage social media platforms.
- Delegating allows businesses to maintain a dynamic online presence and engage with their audience authentically.

- Virtual Assistants can also leverage digital marketing strategies to drive growth and success.
- By embracing this approach, businesses ensure they stay visible and adaptable in an evolving market.
- Focus on Results, Not Methods: allow your team to find their way to achieve the desired results.
- Implementing a KPI-driven result will ensure your VA to work on their focus task, especially in managing social media.

What actions are you going to take from this chapter?

1 _____

_____

_____

_____

_____

2 _____

_____

_____

_____

_____

3 _____

_____

_____

_____

_____

CHAPTER 9

SCALING UP YOUR BUSINESS WITH A VA

∞

Working ON the business…

Now that the Virtual Assistant has taken some responsibilities off your shoulders, you have more time to focus on working ON the business, rather than IN it. I've been reading several books on this topic, which I absolutely love. One book I highly recommend is 'Who Not How' by Dan Sullivan. It has profoundly impacted me, reinforcing my belief in effective delegation–something I pride myself on being exceptionally good at.

Key Takeaways from the Book:
1. **Delegate to the Right People**: instead of asking *"How can I do this?"* focus on *"Who can do this for me?"* to achieve goals more efficiently.
2. **Maximise Strengths**: concentrate on tasks that align with your unique abilities and let others handle areas where they excel.

3. **Multiply Time and Productivity**: by delegating tasks, you free up time to focus on strategic, high-value activities that drive business growth.
4. **Growth Through Collaboration**: genuine success comes from collaborating with others who possess the skills and expertise you lack.
5. **Abundance Mindset**: adopt the belief that there are many skilled individuals who can help you reach your objectives more quickly and effectively.

I love delegation. Delegation is empowering. By passing along tasks, you gain the ability to truly recharge and give back to your team and clients. With fewer daily meetings, you have the opportunity to focus on leadership, strategy, and big-picture thinking.

Learning and implementing...
With more available time, networking becomes a significant avenue for business growth. Being an active member of the Entrepreneur

Organization (EO), I've gained invaluable insights and made connections that significantly influence my business practices. This networking leads to learning opportunities that, in turn, benefit my business exponentially.

With this newfound time, I also engage in creating educational content, such as social media videos and courses. These activities not only enhance my business's visibility but also allow me to share knowledge extensively. For instance, this book I'm writing could not have been possible without the time freed up by delegating routine tasks.

Moreover, I indulge in my hobbies–salsa dancing, beach outings, tennis, and card games–which are vital for my well-being. Being able to nurture my interests helps maintain my happiness and productivity, which are crucial for a successful personal and professional life.

Leveraging Virtual Assistants...

We aim to leverage Virtual Assistants to optimise operations and drive growth, particularly within your sales pipeline. A sales pipeline is essentially a report where the Virtual Assistant logs all leads and their interest in various products. We maintain a distinct pipeline for each product, populated with leads at various stages–from initial interest and curiosity to potentially booking a call, considering the offer, and finally making a decision.

This sales pipeline, which most CRM systems can track effectively, allows us to observe the progression of leads and evaluate the conversion process. Regular business reviews enable us to analyse these pipelines, helping us to address questions such as, *"Last month, we converted this number of leads; this month, the numbers are lower.*

What changed? Are we continuing something that's no longer effective? What adjustments do we need to make to improve our conversion rates?"

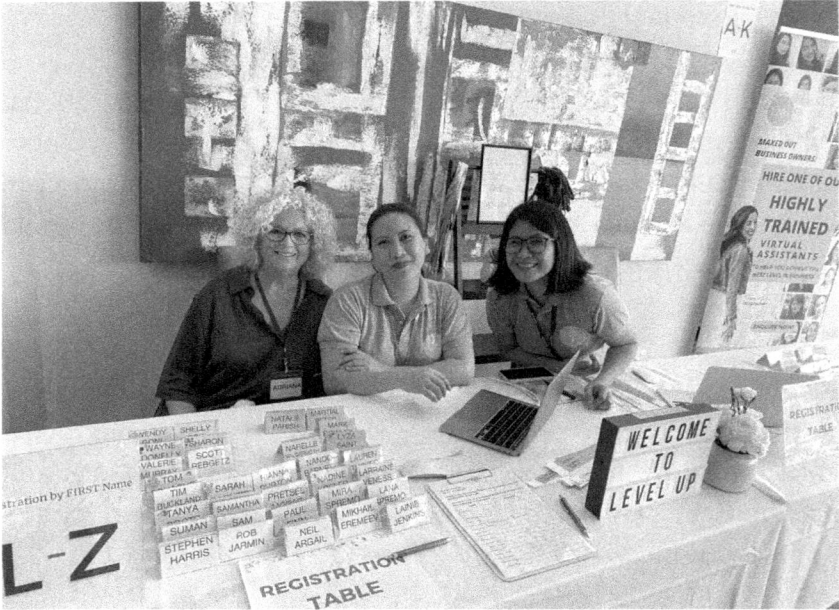

By having the Virtual Assistant regularly report on the sales pipeline during meetings, not only do you gain a detailed understanding of the numbers, but you also ensure the consistency necessary for effective follow-ups. I admit, consistency isn't my strongest suit, and I rely heavily on my Virtual Assistant to keep me on track. Every day, my VA checks the sales pipeline and reminds me of the necessary follow-ups with specific contacts, citing what was discussed during our last interactions. This support is invaluable as it helps us stay organised and ensures no opportunities are missed. This collaborative approach maintains our momentum and drives more effective results, making sure that every lead is nurtured and brought to closure efficiently.

Setting KPIs...

We establish realistic KPIs for our various teams–marketing, administration, customer service–and particularly for those working on lead generation. For my marketing team, for my admin team, for my customer service team.

My team is working on lead generation. They know exactly how many emails they need to get, how many people they need to get into our masterclasses, and how many people they need to book a call with us to buy and become a client. They have realistic KPIs, and they report on these KPIs weekly so that we can stay on top of it and make sure that we measure them.

For customer service, the KPIs include tracking the number of clients we are losing, as client attrition is a normal part of business.

These KPIs are reviewed weekly to ensure we are on target and can measure performance effectively. We need to stay on top of these numbers regularly.

We also set KPIs for email collection, specifying the number of emails my Virtual Assistants need to gather each week and month. Despite my natural resistance to strict KPIs, they are crucial for team accountability. Meeting these KPIs leads to bonuses for the team, fostering motivation and driving excellent results for everyone involved.

Note to self: Incentivise Performance. *Reward and recognise high performance to motivate and retain talent.*

Expanding your Virtual Assistant team...

When and how should more Virtual Assistants be hired? We need to make sure that once we have a VA that helps us not drown, we need to make sure that we don't drown the VA. Deciding when and how to expand your Virtual Assistant team is crucial. Once you have a VA in place to help manage workload, it's important to monitor their capacity closely to prevent them from becoming overwhelmed. This way, we can allow the first VA to teach someone else, so they can focus on their passions and help scale the business to new levels. Recognising when a VA needs support is key to deciding when to hire additional assistance. This allows the initial VA to mentor the new hire, focusing on their strengths and scaling the business to new heights.

Currently, I employ seven full-time VAs, each specialising in areas they excel in, with additional VAs hired to support them. This structure allows every VA the opportunity to advance and specialise further. Many businesses make the mistake of relying on a single VA indefinitely, which can lead to burnout and inefficiency. It's essential to continually assess the distribution of workload and expand your team as needed to maintain a healthy, productive work environment.

When you should hire a VA...

In this chart, you'll be able to see how much we believe the business should be making for you to have one, two to three Virtual Assistants. I don't recommend hiring three VAs all at once. It's sometimes good to have one VA, get used to the business, and then hire a second one. Another thing I noticed people doing is hiring two VAs - one sub aside, so they can learn together. If they are in two different departments and you have staff members who can teach them, that's totally fine, but if you're a one-man band, then it might be hard to stay on top of training two people in the same week.

My focus is this...

Initially, hire one Virtual Assistant who can handle a variety of tasks—essentially a unicorn VA. However, it's common for such a VA to excel more in one area, like marketing, and perhaps be less adept in another, such as administration. When the time comes to expand your team, engage with your VA to identify their preferences and strengths, whether that's in marketing or administrative tasks. This discussion will guide you in hiring a second VA who complements the first by excelling in areas where the first might not be as strong. This strategy allows both VAs to focus on their strengths, supports collaboration, and prevents burnout, ensuring both are performing optimally without being overwhelmed.

Note to self: Collaboration Over Solo Effort. Building a strong team of capable people allows you to focus on your strengths, while others handle tasks that are not your expertise.

Case Study: How Sharon Veness successfully delegated tasks to her VA, Jane

Background

In the journey of life and business, there are pivotal moments that shape our perspectives and approaches. One such transformative lesson is exemplified by Sharon Veness, a Transpersonal Art Therapist and the Founder/CEO of *Sharon Veness Art Therapy*. Before the pandemic, Sharon's innovative art classes were thriving, generating around $7,000 monthly by offering unique transformative experiences through art.

Challenge

When COVID-19 struck, Sharon faced a daunting challenge as her in-person art therapy sessions came to a halt. This sudden disruption jeopardised her steady income and ability to serve clients effectively. Sharon found herself overwhelmed, unable to focus on core business strategies, and missing out on potential growth opportunities. Her personal and professional life balance suffered as she struggled to manage increasing workloads and maintain efficiency.

Solution

To navigate these challenges, Sharon made a crucial decision to hire a Virtual Assistant (VA), Jane. Jane's role was pivotal in transforming Sharon's business operations:

- Delegation and Strategy: Jane handled administrative tasks such as event follow-ups, creating content from live-stream sessions, and editing videos for social media.
- Focused Strategy Implementation: together, they devised a six-week strategy to enhance event participation and engagement.

- Social Media and Online Presence: Jane's efforts significantly boosted Sharon's online presence, leading to increased visibility and client inquiries.

Results

Sharon's proactive approach and collaboration with Jane yielded impressive results:

- Financial Growth: Sharon's monthly income surged to $9,500, a significant increase from pre-pandemic levels, with $20,000 generated in just three months from online workshops.
- Operational Efficiency: with Jane's support, Sharon regained focus on core business activities, achieving higher productivity and scalability.
- Personal Growth: Sharon regained work-life balance, becoming more organised and gaining recognition in her field through enhanced social media presence and successful event management.

Sharon's journey underscores the transformative impact of effective delegation, strategic planning, and leveraging virtual assistance to navigate challenges and achieve sustainable growth in business.

Long term planning and goal setting with your team...

- **Quarterly and Yearly Planning:** it's crucial to focus on long-term objectives. We practice quarterly and yearly planning to ensure everyone is aligned and working toward the same goals.
- **Annual Team Retreat:** we hold an annual team retreat where we all gather to strategise and work on the business. It's not all work, though; we make sure there's plenty of time for fun. This helps strengthen our team dynamic and refreshes everyone's energy.

151

- **Quarterly Managerial Meetings:** regular meetings for the managerial team are essential. These sessions help us stay on top of the business and address any emerging challenges swiftly.

To maintain momentum and ensure continuous improvement, it's important to conduct performance reviews for your Virtual Assistant. This not only helps them grow professionally but also ensures that your business needs are consistently being met.

Note to self: Team Synergy. Teams working together achieve more than individuals working alone.

Key Takeaways

- Working ON the Business: delegating tasks to Virtual Assistants (VAs) gives CEOs more time to focus on strategic growth and leadership rather than daily operations. This shift boosts creativity, productivity, and overall business success.
- Learning and Implementing: by delegating, CEOs can network, learn, and implement new strategies, leading to personal and business growth. More time becomes available for content creation, product development, and expanding business networks.
- Leveraging Virtual Assistants: VAs can manage sales pipelines, ensuring consistent follow-ups and no lost opportunities. Their involvement in operations helps maintain momentum and improves efficiency.
- Setting KPIs: establishing clear KPIs for marketing, admin, and customer service teams provides measurable goals. VAs

help track performance, keeping teams accountable and on target.

- Expanding the VA Team: as your business grows, adding more VAs prevents burnout and ensures efficient task management. Assign VAs according to their strengths and hire others to balance their skills, promoting overall team success.

- When to Hire a VA: hire the first VA when overwhelmed with tasks, and the second when the first reaches capacity. Having multiple VAs ensures coverage during absences and seamless operations.

- Case Study: Sharon Veness grew her business by delegating key tasks to her VA, resulting in increased income, better efficiency, and a stronger online presence.

- Long-Term Planning: regular quarterly and annual planning meetings, as well as performance reviews for VAs, ensure business alignment, accountability, and continuous improvement.

What actions are you going to take from this chapter?

1 _____

_____

_____

_____

2 _____

_____

_____

_____

3 _____

_____

_____

_____

CHAPTER 10

OVERCOMING
CHALLENGES

∞

The greatest challenge I had to overcome when I hired online, as mentioned in the first chapter, was my brain… I had to get my head around hiring someone that wasn't right next to me in the office. I had to learn to be a leader of an online team. But since we have a remote team our business is super strong and all our systems are online.

Literally, it's very similar to hiring locally. We have to praise them and we have to be gentle with our feedback and we have to include them in everyday business occurrences.

The relationship between the CEO and the VA…
In the relationship between a CEO and a Virtual Assistant, there are going to be challenges. It's not going to be all that easy; it will not be all smooth. We're dealing with people - and as we're dealing with people, we need to understand there's going to be ups and

downs, there's going to be times we're unsure if we want to keep them. Times that you are going to question what the VA is actually doing. It's normal. We want to accept that's part of the journey. I know many of us feel this way about local staff members too.

Sometimes it's a pattern of us CEOs, we think we are the only hard working one. But team members will work hard if we guide them and make them feel a vital part of the team.

You and I need to keep in mind that everyone is replaceable (as long as there are procedures in place) but we have to treat them like we don't know that. We have to make them feel unique and irreplaceable. I am not saying we have to lie... we have to know that if anyone leaves is not the end of the world and the show must go on, we will find someone else to do that role and it will all be fine. But while they are employed, we need to treat them like a diamond and look after them. It's all about the small things we do for them to make them feel special. I am not attached to the hours of work. It is ok for my team to take an afternoon off here and there, or to go to their kids' special event at school. I want them to feel free as long as when they are working, they are super productive and they help the business move forward.

Some of us, myself included, realise what we should have done better only when it's too late. By then, we've 'broken' our VA, lost their commitment, and brought out their worst. But don't panic–it's not the end. There's still a chance to repair the relationship. And if we can't, we need to recognise that letting go may be the best decision for both us and the VA.

I did that with one of my first VAs. She joined the team remotely when there was only me and her. I burnt her out and then I tried to give her support and hire other people (a little too late). By then she was addicted to do it all, to the buzz, to be the only person I could count on, so subconsciously she never trained the other VAs on the things that needed to be done. She kept all the most important things, because she genuinely believed she was the only one she could trust to do the job.

I heard something in a podcast by Brooke Castillo that I will never forget… When the business is in the early stages, we often hire people to put out fires. We need someone quick at finding solutions and implementing them. We train them in that fast-paced environment, and without realising, we get them addicted to the adrenaline of the urgent, last-minute vibe. When the business grows and we don't need that anymore, those employees struggle because they are searching for the endorphins that the business used to give them.Sometimes those team members end up creating the fires so they can put them out… not healthy for the business.

My initial Virtual Assistant eventually began underperforming during slower periods. She would make so many more mistakes when things were going smoothly, and she became the bottle neck of the business. I was unable to salvage that relationship. She had to eventually go and put out fires somewhere else so that she could feel useful.

Note to self: Shared Ownership. *Empower others by giving them ownership over their responsibilities.*

How do you know if you've broke your VA?

It's one of the topics we wanted to discuss because I was reading a book on this, specifically in romantic relationships–how many of us, as women, unintentionally break men apart. I find that concept fascinating. The book, *The Queen's Code*, by Alison Armstrong, explores this idea in depth.

In that book, she explained how a lot of women find a prince and then turn the prince into a frog. They call it frog farming. By emasculating a man and trying to control him by telling him what to do, by belittling him in front of his friends, or by manipulating him to get what they want.

I think that a lot of us CEOs do that frog farming with our staff. The VAs are these amazing unicorns that come through our businesses, and they are keen, they are engaged and then we break them. Then we complain about how the VA did this, and the VA did that, rather than looking at how we contributed to frog farming the VA.

If we train them, support them, empower them, they will not break. They're not going to be dismissive; they're not going to disappear on us, and they're not going to ghost us. None of that will happen if we are committed and if we do the right thing by our team.

What is considered "frog farming a VA"?

Frog farming a VA refers to setting them up for failure by expecting too much too soon, without proper guidance or support. It's when you hire someone but fail to provide the necessary tools, training, or communication they need to thrive. In essence, it's treating the VA as if they should instinctively know how to handle everything without your involvement, which leads to frustration and disappointment on both sides.

Are you expecting your VA to run the business without putting in any effort to build the relationship? Are you expecting them to be a mind reader, knowing exactly what you want and how you want it done, without clear guidance?

If we haven't taken the time to train our VA and explain their tasks, we can't expect them to excel. Outstanding performance only comes after we've invested time in their training and set clear expectations.

Frog farming is a serious thing. A lot of us as business owners are time-poor, and we often think, *"Let me just quickly send these couple of notes to my VA,"* and expect the VA to do the task from a half-explained note, without allowing them to ask any questions. Then the VA will come back to us asking for feedback, but we don't have time, so we ignore the VA. And then, two weeks later, we're like, *"Have you done that thing that I asked you?"* And the VA is like, *"Yeah, I gave it to you for you to check,"* and then you realise you haven't checked it. GUILTY here! I have done this soooo many times (Face Palm!)

And then you get annoyed and frustrated, right? (I did! Face Palm)

I've done that too. This pattern happens especially to those types of business owners that are like me, the creator type.

Frog Farming a VA has three major steps:
1. Ignoring a VA
2. Drowning a VA
3. Losing our Passion

1. Ignoring a VA...

So how does someone break a VA? Number one, by ignoring them. You are not showing up for meetings or cancelling them last minute. You are not supporting them and not answering their questions. Avoiding your VA is the first way to break them. And if you continue doing that, your VA will disconnect, and it's hard to bring them back on board and get them excited about the business again.

I remember this client of mine, very successful business, and the CEO is a creator type, lots of ideas and very little free time, often rushing and often late. This CEO would go weeks without speaking to the VA, and then, out of nowhere, would demand something urgent with almost no explanation or background on the task. This approach was essentially setting the VA up for failure, as they had no clear direction or understanding of the task. It's a perfect example of how poor communication can overwhelm a VA and prevent them from doing their best work..

Every VA we found this client would feel burned out within two months and wanted to quit. The VA didn't understand their role and didn't know what was expected from them. We tried to coach the CEO to slow down to go faster, but some people aren't ready to hear this concept. So, they kept losing all the VAs as nobody could work in a highly stressful environment, and they kept getting new VAs to train, which was a waste of time for his business. Eventually the client understood that if they didn't change, no one could survive in their business.

2. Drowning the VA...

Another common issue is overloading the VA with too many tasks, which can drown them. People often fail to slow down and teach them everything they need to know, assuming the VA will figure it out on their own once they know everything that needs to be done. This approach leads to overwhelming the VA and can ultimately cause problems, which is not ideal.

My beautiful VA Vine is here live with me, listening while I speak out this book, yes, we are on Zoom, I speak out this book and then she will transcribe it and edit it…. And as I'm creating the content for this book, I'm going to now ask my beautiful VA to write down the three steps that I just mentioned, so that I can repeat them back to you. Because I'm a creator, I most likely have already forgotten points one and two, as I speak.. So it's important for me to have that support and I always leveraged on my beautiful VA that is now going to write what I just said two minutes ago. There we go. My VA just reminded me number one was ignoring the VA and number two drowning the VA. We are moving on to step 3, which is losing our passion. Everything I do, especially content wise, I have my VA on Zoom with me to help me avoid mistakes.

3. Losing our passion…

When we are losing our passion for our own business, we become contagious. So whatever we do, the VAs will mirror us. When we lose passion for the business, we stop showing up consistently, fail to plan ahead, and neglect strategies to attract new clients. I had a client who felt lost and uncertain about whether they wanted to continue their business. In the meantime, the VA was trying to keep things afloat, but the client slowly started to disappear, engaging less and less. It got to the point where, for 3-4 weeks, the client didn't communicate with the VA at all. Later, the client felt disappointed with the VA, questioning what they had done during that time, unaware of the lack of direction they had provided. The VA became demotivated because when leadership is absent, the team feels it. We can't blame the VA for disengaging when we haven't been present.

It's our responsibility to keep the energy and spirit high, and that starts with strong leadership.

Have you done any of these things? Have you avoided your VA? Have you drowned your VA with all the tasks they need to do? Have you lost your passion for your business, which means the VA is now mirroring your energy? If any of these things happen, you have broken your VA. This means it's going to be really hard, and you will need to spend a lot of energy to get your VA to buy back in and get the momentum back.

We are most likely the cause of why the VA is not that proactive and productive now. Did they used to be very good in the beginning? And now they're not doing that well? What did you do to them? Or what happened along the way?

So how do we unbreak a VA?

Now, if you know for sure that your VA was broken by you, then you need to make sure that you come up with a way to re-engage your virtual assistant.

1. Re-Engagement Call:
So, the re-engagement call looks like this. *"Hey Jenny, Thank you for jumping on a call with me. I wanted to let you know I have been on a journey over the last few months, and during these months, I was struggling. I know I didn't give you much attention, and I didn't really support you much. I'm so sorry that I haven't helped or supported you in the business, and I've left you to your own device, which you've been amazing at. I've noticed that lately, you're not as engaged because I wasn't, and you're a reflection of me. I'm so sorry if I didn't show up as the boss you deserve. But listen, I see you, and I saw how amazing you*

were, especially at the beginning. I want that VA back, and to have that VA back, I know I need to step up. So here I am, stepping up, admitting my mistakes, and apologising for what I've done. I promise to do everything I can to avoid repeating my past mistakes. I'm here to work through this together. I would love to start working on the things you want to focus on. We're going to tackle one project at a time, together. We'll have regular calls—please put them in my calendar. Let's keep me accountable. Let's do this together. I believe you're the right VA for me, and I'm sorry if I didn't show up as the right CEO for you. But from now on, I'm all in. Are you?"

And then you let the VA buy in. This is the first thing you want to do so that when your VA is excited, you're excited, and you're back on board, right?

2. Follow Through:
Number two is don't mess it up now. Number two is literally to follow through—follow through on your promise, and make sure that you do everything you can to follow through. This is vital. Because if you now have done a re-engagement call and then if you don't follow through, the VA is going to be like, *"I don't want to work with someone who doesn't stick to their word, right? It's not fun, it's not inspiring, I just don't like it."*

So, whatever you need to do, put it in your calendar, ask a VA to keep you accountable, show up, just do everything you can to stick to your word.

3. Break Things Down into Small Projects:
Number three is breaking tasks down into small projects. So, take one project at a time and work with your VA together on a *Zoom* call. This fosters collaboration and builds a stronger relationship.

You and your VA will start working together on tasks, and in doing so, you'll strengthen both your relationship and your business. This step is vital. What often happens is that business owners try to follow through on promises but still work too independently–and that doesn't work.

Stay consistent with your promises, hop on regular calls, and work on projects together. Truly collaborate. When you do this, you'll see excitement and engagement come back, and that's when you know you're on the right track.

Handling Issues with VAs and Conflict Resolution

One common characteristic of most Virtual Assistants is their dedication to their jobs, often stemming from a fear of losing their position. They would go to great lengths to ensure job security. From the outset, I make it clear to all Virtual Assistants that no mistake is a deal breaker, except for dishonesty. We should not view mistakes as reasons to immediately dismiss a VA. Instead, we should address issues constructively and not sever ties over a simple human error.

What to Do When a VA Makes a Mistake: Before any mistake occurs, it's crucial to set expectations about handling errors. Inform them about the approach you expect them to take and how they should react to effectively resolve the issue. Here's how I typically handle such situations:

"Firstly, don't panic. It's okay to make mistakes; it's part of being human. If you make a mistake, take a breath, come straight to me, and tell me the truth. Explain what went wrong and bring three possible solutions.

Do nothing until I've helped you understand which solution is best and why. Together, we'll work on fixing the mistake."

1. **Understanding the Root Cause:** once we've resolved the immediate issue, it's important to delve into why the mistake occurred, not to blame but to prevent future occurrences. This involves a thorough discussion, perhaps over *Zoom*, where we explore whether a procedure was in place or forgotten. We discuss:

   "Did you follow the existing procedure? Did you forget about it? If you forgot, how can we ensure it doesn't happen again? Should you review the procedure monthly? Perhaps we need to create a Standard Operating Checklist (SOC) to make it easier to follow? Maybe the mistake stemmed from a new or outdated step in the procedure? Is it something that only happens occasionally?"

   By understanding the underlying cause of the mistake and discussing it openly, we ensure better preparation for the future, significantly reducing the likelihood of repeat issues. This collaborative approach not only resolves problems but also strengthens trust and efficiency within the team.

2. **Not Meeting Deadlines:** another common challenge with Virtual Assistants is not meeting deadlines. To prevent this, help them break down the project into manageable phases and schedule each step in the calendar. It's crucial to clarify your expectations right from the start and require regular weekly updates on the project. This fosters clear communication and team cohesion, enabling you to work together to meet deadlines. This clarity and teamwork help

ensure deadlines are met. After repeating this process a few times, the VA will understand how to manage and progress projects smoothly.

3. **VA Being Late:** a Virtual Assistant is late, it's essential to approach this issue with understanding rather than frustration. Discuss why they are late and whether adjustments to their schedule might help, such as starting an hour later. The goal is to set up conditions for their success, ensuring punctuality and respect for each other's time. If a Virtual Assistant is consistently late, it's not about getting upset or angry; it's about understanding the reason behind it. If timing is an issue, perhaps they need to start an hour later each day? It's about setting them up for success and understanding their needs, rather than punishing mistakes.

4. **Virtual Assistants Not Being Responsive:** often, if a VA becomes unresponsive, it might be a sign we've failed to keep them engaged or have overlooked their growth needs. I make it a point to check in with my Virtual Assistant daily, assigning new tasks and ensuring there's no repetition that could lead to boredom. It's crucial to keep introducing them to exciting projects to maintain their interest and prevent them from looking elsewhere. Without variety, they may become bored and look for opportunities elsewhere.

5. **Dropping Balls:** sometimes, a VA might start dropping the ball on tasks they previously handled well. We need to look into why this is happening—is it boredom, or is nobody checking their work? It's crucial to engage and interact with your Virtual Assistant regularly to keep them focused and responsive.

6. **Virtual Assistant Not Being Consistent:** this is a challenge I've faced for years, and it always makes me wonder, why isn't someone consistent? Often, if they're bored, their performance starts to waver. Excitement for a new project might cause them to neglect other responsibilities. This is why holding regular performance reviews is crucial, to emphasise that consistency is a non-negotiable part of their role. We must make it clear that consistency can't be compromised and should be a priority in their daily tasks.

7. **VA Being a People Pleaser.** Many Virtual Assistants, particularly those we work with from the Philippines, are naturally inclined to say *"yes ma'am"* or *"yes sir,"* and they often struggle to say no. They might agree to tasks even if they're overwhelmed, which can lead to unmet expectations and disappointment. I always encourage my team to be realistic and honest about what they can achieve. I tell them, *"Tell me what you can realistically accomplish in the next two weeks,"* rather than over promising and under delivering. This tendency to please can set both the assistant and our working relationship up for failure. If a VA consistently fails to meet their commitments, it erodes trust, and you might find yourself questioning their reliability in the future, potentially leading you to micromanage. To prevent these issues, it's crucial from the start to establish clear communication and set proper expectations. For those already working with a VA, discuss these dynamics and establish protocols to foster honesty and realistic goal-setting. If you're just starting out, lay these foundations early to avoid potential pitfalls.

8. **Handling Issues Trust, Security and Confidentiality:** security is crucial, but there are tools to enhance it. An antivirus is essential, and there are programs like *Time Doctor* that monitor work by taking screenshots throughout the day. For password management, *1Password* is excellent as it helps with sharing passwords temporarily or securely transferring credentials. Yet, despite these tools, the fundamental issue remains trust. It's paramount, and while tools can provide security, they don't replace the need to trust your Virtual Assistants.

You have to trust your VAs, unless they give you a reason not to, especially if they come through a reliable agency. We perform extensive checks on our Virtual Assistants and their work locations to ensure reliability. Over a decade of hiring VAs, I've faced minimal issues. Security consciousness has grown over the years; I used to share passwords via Excel, but now prefer *1Password* for safer sharing. I opt to trust unless given a reason otherwise, which isn't just about easing operational processes–it's about enabling them to fully contribute to the workload. Trusting them to manage crucial aspects of your work, like social media, involves risk, but it's a calculated one that I'm comfortable with. Ultimately, the extent to which you share sensitive information depends on your comfort with risk and the trustworthiness of your VA.

Note to self: *Delegating Ownership: Let others take full ownership of their responsibilities.*

Strategies for Providing Effective Feedback and Managing Performance.

When providing feedback and managing performance, it's crucial to ensure the communication is direct and personal:

- **Zoom Calls for Feedback:** this allows for a more personal and effective conversation where nuances can be better understood and addressed.
- **Reassurance:** begin each session by reassuring the Virtual Assistant that they are not in trouble. This sets a positive tone and opens up a space for honest and productive feedback.
- **Quarterly Performance Reviews:** conduct these reviews every quarter to assess and manage performance systematically. Before the review, ask the VA to fill out a form detailing their recent activities, challenges, and accomplishments. This helps in preparing for a structured discussion.
- **Engagement in Reviews:** while our clients typically aren't involved in this internal process, it's essential for maintaining

the quality of our service. These reviews help ensure that both you and your Virtual Assistant are content with the workflow and their contributions.

By following these strategies, we aim to maintain a transparent, supportive, and efficient working relationship with all our Virtual Assistants, ensuring both their growth and the success of your operations.

Note to self: Consistent Feedback Loops. *Maintain regular feedback loops with your team to ensure continued alignment.*

Key Takeaways:

- Transitioning to leading a remote team requires a mindset shift, but it can strengthen business systems and operations.
- Maintaining a strong relationship with your Virtual Assistant (VA) involves praise, gentle feedback, and inclusiveness in daily tasks.
- Leadership in a remote setting comes with challenges, but consistency, communication, and guidance can resolve uncertainties.
- VAs can only thrive if empowered with ownership, training, and clear expectations; neglecting these will lead to disengagement.
- CEOs often mistakenly overburden themselves, forgetting that with the right support and trust, their team will work just as hard.
- Treating VAs with respect, making them feel unique, and offering flexibility can keep them motivated and productive.

- Mistreatment, such as "frog farming" VAs by overwhelming them without support or ignoring their needs, leads to their disengagement.
- If a CEO loses passion, the team, including the VA, mirrors this energy, leading to reduced performance and commitment.
- A re-engagement call can revive a broken relationship with a VA, but consistent follow-through on promises is key to success.
- Providing tools like proper training, regular check-ins, and constructive feedback ensures a VA's long-term success and loyalty.

What actions are you going to take from this chapter?

1 _____

_____

_____

_____

_____

2 _____

_____

_____

_____

_____

3 _____

_____

_____

_____

_____

CHAPTER 11

WORK AND DELEGATION

∞

They are saying that AI is going to replace Virtual Assistants. I don't believe that's true. I believe that AI, like any other innovation in the world, will help us and support us in taking this collaboration to the next level but it will not replace human beings. A simple example I can give you is when we had factories and decided to create machines for the tasks that men and women were doing manually. The machines didn't really replace the men and women. The men became supervisors and ensured that nothing went wrong with the machines. They still had to do something manually to make sure that the machine is doing the right thing. It's the same with Virtual Assistants; they are always going to be there.

They're going to have different skills and knowledge, but it's not going to ever replace them completely. And we want to make sure that we understand AI and leverage it. We need to use it to do all the things we need to, because AI is powerful; if we don't use it, we'll be left behind by those leveraging AI for their business. We need to stay aware of the emerging trends in the virtual world, and since we're doing remote work, we must ensure we stay on top of those trends. I have a virtual system that is going to do this, looking at all the different platforms and tools available to help us work faster. We'll make the virtual system work faster and more efficiently.

We can always save time; it's all about being on top of trends so that we can save time. As business owners, we have to stay on top of the latest trends. One of the things we're going to share with you is *Canva*. *Canva AI* is a suite of tools within *Canva* that leverages artificial intelligence to simplify design tasks. It offers features like:

- **Magic Resize**: which instantly adapts designs to various dimensions.
- **Magic Write**: which generates text content. *Canva AI* also includes background remover, colour palette suggestions, and automated design layouts.
- **Text to Image**: generate unique images based on text prompts, which are perfect for creating custom visuals quickly.
- **Magic Edit**: edit photos with AI, adjusting elements like colour, brightness, and more, without needing advanced editing skills.
- **Magic Eraser**: remove unwanted objects from images seamlessly.
- **Beat Sync**: Automatically sync music tracks to video edits, making video creation smoother.
- **Translate**: instantly translate text within your designs to different languages, broadening your content's reach.
- **Style Transfer**: apply artistic styles to photos or designs, mimicking famous art styles with just one click.
- **Brand Kit**: AI helps maintain brand consistency by automatically applying your brand colours, fonts, and logos across all designs.

For business owners and VAs, *Canva AI* boosts productivity by speeding up the design process, allowing quicker creation of marketing materials, social media posts, and presentations. It eliminates the need for deep design skills, enabling VAs to efficiently handle design tasks, freeing up more time for strategic business activities.

Another one is the *ChatGPT Explore*. It's a feature designed to help users dive deeper into specific topics, providing enhanced insights and tailored information. It offers detailed explanations, context, and examples, making it ideal for those who want to explore subjects more thoroughly while maintaining a conversational and accessible style.

The bottom line of having an agency is that we do that for our clients; we teach a Virtual Assistant the latest news trends and applications to fast-track their success and save them time. They can be even more productive for our clients.

My biggest suggestion is to make sure that you hire someone through an agency. And another option is to put them through courses and training, and there are a lot of them out there. Stay innovative by continuously learning and developing both yourself and your Virtual Assistants. Use resources like *LinkedIn* training, books, and online courses, but have your Virtual Assistants summarise them for efficiency. Attend networking events to stay updated on industry trends. Invest in self-development and keep your virtual team informed about emerging technologies shaping the future of virtual assistance. This approach ensures growth, prevents stagnation, and maintains your leadership edge.

There's always new technology, and if we don't stay on top of it, the business will fall behind. Our competitors will be doing it. Even though sometimes we can get stuck in our old ways, I've always done it this way: we need to make sure that we stay on top of the trends. The other day, I was talking to a friend of mine. He was telling me that he quit his job because he was working for this buyer's agent who was not up to the technology they didn't have; they were still doing contracts manually because he didn't trust *DocuSign*. They were still filling out forms and asking for feedback manually. You have got to stay up to date; you have to do things faster. Filling out forms manually is something that I can't do; I don't like it when I go to places where they ask me to fill out a form, and I have to write it down. If we don't stay updated with technology and fail to adapt our skills, businesses won't survive. It's crucial to embrace changes, starting with the basics. Neglecting small advancements will lead us to fall behind, particularly with the role of AI and automation in the worlds of delegation and Virtual Assistants.

Note to self: Use Technology. *Leverage technology and software to automate processes wherever possible.*

Key Takeaways

- AI and VAs: AI will not replace Virtual Assistant s but will enhance their roles. Like machines in factories, AI assists, but human oversight remains crucial. VAs will adapt to new skills and tools to stay relevant.
- Staying Ahead with AI: business owners and VAs must embrace AI, such as *Canva AI* and *ChatGPT Explore*, to save time and boost efficiency. Tools like these simplify tasks, allowing more focus on strategic growth.
- Continuous Learning: to remain competitive, it's essential to stay updated on emerging trends and technologies. Investing in training and development for both business owners and VAs ensures ongoing growth and innovation.
- Embracing Change: refusing to adopt new technologies risks falling behind competitors. Keeping up with advancements is vital to maintain efficiency and business success in a rapidly evolving digital landscape.

What actions are you going to take from this chapter?

1 _____

_____

_____

_____

_____

2 _____

_____

_____

_____

_____

3 _____

_____

_____

_____

_____

CHAPTER 12

TEAM PERSPECTIVES: OUR JOURNEY

∞

In this book, I talked a lot about my relationship with my team from my point of view. But it's not about me! My team were the ones that have contributed to my business and my life so much! I wanted them to have the opportunity to tell you about them and how it is to work in a business that is working with remote staff. You will start hearing from Lina my, Client Relationship manager – she is here in Brisbane with me working from the office Tuesday to Thursday and from home Mondays and Fridays. Lina's dream was to spend three months each year working from Colombia, and what better company to help her achieve that than ours, with a predominantly remote team? We understand the flexibility and freedom remote work offers, which makes our company the perfect fit for someone with dreams like Lina's. By embracing a remote-first culture, we're able to support the personal and professional aspirations of our team members while still driving success in the business.

Then you will hear from Bebs, my EA and financial officer. Bebs is based in the Philippines but has been in Brisbane over three times now and from now on it will be even more often. And then you will hear from the rest of my team: Maria, Dee, Vine, Joann and Rei.

Enjoy ☺

Lina's POV

Hello, I'm Lina. I am the Client Service Manager of EVS, I work in the Brisbane's office with the CEO Francesca Moi. Before joining Empowering Virtual Solution (EVS), I practised as a corporate lawyer within Colombia's oil and gas sector and later worked in various capacities within small to medium enterprises in Australia. Joining EVS marked a significant shift in my career trajectory, not only because I transitioned industries but also because it introduced me to the dynamic world of virtual assistance.

Initially, the prospect of working closely with a virtual team rather than in a traditional office setting seemed daunting. I had always thrived in environments bustling with colleagues, and the thought of relying primarily on remote support presented a new challenge. However, inspired by Francesca's vision and leadership, I embraced the role, eager to explore innovative ways of working.

The impact of integrating Virtual Assistants into our workflow was transformative. Far from the isolation I feared, I found incredible support in our VAs. They brought a fresh, objective perspective to every task and challenge, offering insights and actions that were both effective and enlightening. Their ability to manage situations from afar was not just a relief; it was a revelation, showcasing the power of remote collaboration.

Our VAs are exceptionally skilled–both technically and interpersonally. In my experience, the level of support and efficiency they bring to daily operations has set a new standard for teamwork. They are not just assistants; they are integral parts of our team, driving success through their dedication and expertise. I cannot envision a working environment without their presence now; I have never felt more supported in a role than in this one.

Our agency not only alleviates the workload for busy entrepreneurs and growing organisations but also significantly enhances the quality of life for our VAs in the Philippines.

By enabling them to work from home, we offer them a respite from the gruelling daily commutes that are all too common in their country. This shift not only supports their work-life balance but also fosters a vibrant community of virtual professionals who support each other just as much as they support our clients.

I am immensely proud to be part of an organisation that not only impacts businesses positively but also cares deeply for its team members' well-being. If you're considering a change or need additional support, I wholeheartedly recommend trying out a Virtual Assistant. It's more than a convenience–it's a game-changer, both for your business and for the lives of those who help carry your vision forward.

Beb's POV

Hello everyone! I'm Bebs, and I've been navigating the vibrant world of virtual assistance with Francesca Moi since 2017. Transitioning from a structured corporate life to the dynamic realm of a Virtual Assistant was filled with unexpected turns and invaluable lessons.

When I was introduced to the VA role, it was out of sheer necessity during a transitional phase in my life. The flexibility it offered seemed like a perfect fit for my situation, allowing me to manage my professional responsibilities alongside personal commitments. Francesca, or FM as we affectionately call her, saw potential in me during a time when I was questioning my professional direction.

Starting as FM's part-time VA while maintaining my corporate job posed significant challenges, especially in managing my time effectively. My initial weeks were tough, juggling two demanding roles, which eventually led to a brief termination due to schedule conflicts.

However, determined to prove my worth, I continued to work secretly, refining my skills in social media coordination, graphic design, and client communication. This persistence paid off when Francesca discovered my continued efforts and rehired me, a moment that significantly boosted my confidence and commitment to this path.

Opting to turn down a full-time VA role initially, I continued to enhance my skills discreetly. My dedication culminated in accepting a full-time position nine months later, a decision that marked the true beginning of my transformative journey with EVS.

I became FM's temp Executive Assistant (EA), I handle a plethora of tasks that streamline her day-to-day operations. From managing her calendar and cleaning up her emails to ensuring her inbox hits zero at the end of the day, my role is pivotal. I also oversee her speaking engagements, manage bookings for her Airbnb, and assist our finance department with critical tasks like updating sales KPIs, managing subscriptions, and handling invoicing. Beyond administrative tasks, I took on the responsibility of managing our payroll system, overseeing timesheets, and ensuring all VAs were compensated timely, reflecting my commitment to the team's welfare. These initiatives alone reduce our operational cost by almost 2K weekly.

But my role extends beyond just administrative tasks. I lead a team of 13 VAs, supervising and mentoring them to ensure that they not only meet but exceed our client's expectations.

We foster a supportive environment where VAs can share their victories and challenges, enhancing our collective growth and ensuring continuity in client satisfaction. My interactions with the VAs aren't just about overseeing their tasks; they're about engaging with them in a way that helps them brainstorm and enhance their approach to client work. This not only improves their performance but also directly benefits our clients' businesses. The reason why some of my clients onboard a second and third VA is because of the endless support of EVS not just for their VAs but for their clientele too.

This journey has taught me the invaluable lessons of resilience, continuous improvement, and the profound impact effective support can have on a business's operations. My evolution from a tentative newcomer to a confident leader within EVS highlights the transformative power of dedicated Virtual Assistants.

The opportunity to work alongside FM and contribute to structuring our clients' businesses has not only been a professional achievement but also a personal triumph. This project alone contributed almost 20K in sales on FM's business and another 10K-24K annually on grants approved for the business. It's a testament to how virtual assistance can transcend traditional job roles, offering flexibility and growth opportunities that are hard to find in more conventional settings.

As I reflect on my journey, I am profoundly grateful for the experiences and growth opportunities afforded by my role at EVS. For anyone considering integrating a VA into their business, let my story inspire you: the right VA can bring unparalleled efficiency, innovation, and transformation to your operations, empowering not just your business but also the lives of those involved.

Maria's POV

Hello! I'm Maria, one of Francesca Moi's dedicated Virtual Assistants, and I've been with her since 2020. Let me share my transformative journey with you. Before joining EVS, my business experience was confined to running a small snack shop next to a school. My digital skills were basic, limited to personal use of social platforms like *Facebook*, *Instagram*, *TikTok*, and *YouTube*.

The turning point came unexpectedly during the pandemic when I received a call from my sister, who worked for EVS. She surprised me with an opportunity I hadn't even sought myself–I was going to become a Virtual Assistant! Though new to this field, my excitement to learn outweighed my inexperience.

Joining EVS opened a world of endless learning. I mastered various digital tools and applications essential for today's businesses, significantly enhancing my time management and organisational skills. More importantly, I learned the critical importance of attention to detail and adaptability–skills that proved vital as I navigated my responsibilities.

Initially, I was tasked with managing client information across platforms like *Ontraport*, *Airtable*, and *WordPress*. The stakes were high, and the fear of making a mistake was real–especially when the 'edit' button was perilously close to 'delete'. This experience taught me to be meticulous and always double-check my work.

Creating social media content and interacting with clients initially pushed me out of my comfort zone. To overcome this, I immersed myself in learning from top mentors and participating in groups like Tony Robbins' Ultimate Breakthrough Challenge to better understand the mindset required for success.

My confidence grew as I started managing relationships–one client and VA at a time. From my first client interaction in October 2022 to now overseeing 11 clients and 9 VAs, my approach has always been gradual but steady, allowing me to build confidence and refine my skills over time.

Today, my role has expanded to include updating client data, creating engaging content like PDFs, blogs, and reports, training interns, and supervising a growing team of VAs. My KPIs focus on gathering client feedback and enhancing participation in our monthly CEO coaching calls, targets I strive to meet consistently.

2024 marked a milestone in my professional growth. Francesca provided us with an incredible opportunity to travel from the Philippines to Australia, where I not only experienced an office setup but also played a pivotal role in our biggest event of the year, the Level Up Business Conference. This experience transformed me from an introvert to a confident networker.

One of the most rewarding outcomes of my role at EVS is the financial stability it has brought to my family. As a single parent, I've been able to support my son through college and contribute to building our family home—a dream come true.

My journey with EVS has been nothing short of life-changing. From a humble snack vendor to a confident Virtual Assistant making substantial impacts, I've embraced the challenges and opportunities that have come my way. I am excited about what the future holds and am ready to tackle more challenges and continue my growth trajectory with EVS.

Dee's POV

Hello! I'm Dee, and for over five years, I have been part of the dynamic team at Empowering Virtual Solution (EVS). My journey here has been a blend of continuous learning and essential adaptations, underscored by the crucial role of effective communication.

Initially, I joined as a Marketing VA, where my primary duties included enhancing our social media presence, securing organic bookings, and managing the logistics for our active schedule of events. My position was multifaceted: I was not only promoting these events but also ensuring every booking was precisely recorded and all attendees were promptly reminded. Essentially, I served as the Social Media Coordinator and the Event Filling Person. This role was pivotal–without attendees at the events, our CEO couldn't showcase or sell our products and services, which are the lifeblood of our business model.

However, my responsibilities expanded dramatically overnight when a colleague unexpectedly left. I found myself managing both the front-end and back-end marketing operations. This transition demanded swift adaptation as I took on backend tasks like campaign automation and email management–areas I was initially unfamiliar with.

How did I navigate this shift? The foundation of my approach was solid communication combined with stringent time management. By setting clear expectations, establishing firm boundaries, and maintaining open lines of communication with my team, I mastered these new responsibilities. This process also sharpened my skills in navigating various technical platforms essential to our operations.

Despite the increased workload, I successfully met our ambitious marketing targets, achieving monthly KPIs that include 60 online masterclass bookings, 40 face-to-face event bookings, and 4 game-changer calls. These achievements highlight the importance of adaptability and teamwork in a high-stakes environment.

Furthermore, my expanded role involved supervising other VAs and managing client interactions–tasks that require precision and acute attention to detail. Managing these diverse responsibilities emphasised the necessity of effective time management, which not only fostered professional growth but also personal development, allowing me to maintain a work-life balance, a cornerstone of EVS' philosophy.

At EVS, we don't just work; we grow and thrive together. The support and flexibility here have enabled me to enhance my professional skills while still enjoying precious moments with my family. It's a testament to the environment that Francesca has nurtured–one that values each team member's contribution and ensures that even as we push for professional excellence, we never lose sight of what matters most.

In conclusion, my role at EVS has transformed me from a diligent worker into a multifaceted professional capable of managing complex tasks with ease. For anyone considering integrating a VA into their business, let my journey be your assurance: the right VA can bring unparalleled efficiency and innovation to your operations, especially in critical areas like event management that directly impact your business's bottom line.

Vine's POV

Hi there! I'm Vine, one of Francesca Moi's dedicated Virtual Assistants at Empowering Virtual Solution. Since joining in 2019, my journey has been both dynamic and deeply fulfilling, evolving from a Marketing VA to a VA Supervisor. My primary role involves enhancing our clients' and our own marketing strategies, implementing innovative plans, and ensuring our approach is as dynamic and effective as possible.

Working at EVS for nearly five years, I've seen firsthand how setting clear and challenging goals, like securing 5-8 sales calls per month for our agency, can drive significant growth. My personal strategy involves connecting with 20 high-level business owners weekly on *LinkedIn* using a carefully crafted script that converts these connections into valuable sales opportunities.

As the handler of the Business Behind the Scene podcast and reels video recordings, I play a pivotal role in content creation—a task our CEO, FM, prefers to delegate. I manage everything from planning our Video Content Plan in *Airtable* to coordinating the recording sessions. On recorded *Zoom* meetings of max one hour (that is as much as I can keep FM's attention for ☺), I ensure everything is set for FM to deliver her best, from warming up with a brief chat to executing a marathon session where we record up to 20 videos to cover our monthly social media needs.

My expertise doesn't stop at podcasting and videos. I'm also proficient in using *LinkedIn* for lead generation, crafting newsletters, and organising event promotions. These efforts are crucial in growing our audience and converting interest into active engagement and attendance at our events.

On the creative front, I guide our clients and fellow VAs on producing high-quality, on-brand videos that are not only trendy but also impactful. My guidance covers everything from selecting the right topics to the finer points of video editing, ensuring that every piece of content not only resonates with the audience but also opens up avenues for monetisation.

Being a Marketing VA and Supervisor at EVS has been an incredible journey of growth and learning. I've gained so much knowledge and experience, not just from my own efforts but also from the amazing people I work with.

To our wonderful leader, Francesca Moi, thank you for the opportunity to grow alongside you and the EVS team. As I continue to evolve and contribute to EVS, my goal remains clear: to help our business and our clients achieve unprecedented success. The journey here is about pushing boundaries and embracing challenges–and I am here for it all, ready to take on more and contribute to our collective success.

Joann's POV

Hello! I'm Joann, one of Francesca's dedicated VA since 2021. Coming from a completely different industry. (I work in a hospital for 12 years) I took a significant risk by deciding to become a Virtual Assistant. Initially, it was challenging, but EVS provided me with all the necessary support to help me grow. I have developed my skills, mainly in communication, and gained expertise in areas I never thought possible. The most important lesson I've learned about working effectively as a Virtual Assistant is that with the right support and training, growth and improvement are always possible. At EVS, we delegate a wide range of tasks to VAs to ensure the smooth operation of the business. These tasks include Admin support, Customer service, Marketing support, Sales assistant and more.

During my first year with EVS, I encountered multiple challenges. One significant challenge arose when one of our team members went on maternity leave. This sudden shift required me to step up and take on additional responsibilities, pushing me to adapt and learn new skills quickly. I was hesitant at first, feeling unprepared, but aside from the marketing tasks, we built a new business, and as VAs, we had to step up as supervisors. Despite the overwhelming workload, I focused on developing my skills to work more efficiently. To overcome these challenges, I leveraged the resources and courses available at EVS, as well as *YouTube* and Google.

As a Virtual Assistant and Sales Assistant, my role is vital to the success of EVS. I play a crucial part in supporting the sales team.

I ensure that the sales team operates efficiently and that our clients receive the best possible service. My responsibilities include Lead generation, messaging people, managing Sales pipeline and staying on top of our leads to follow up. Every day, I update our sales pipeline; my strategy is to summarise all leads that need follow-up with a little note and necessary details like number, email or messenger link so FM can easily do follow-ups in just five minutes! I also use my calendar for follow up reminders to make sure we don't miss any opportunities. We aim for 20 sales calls a month and convert 10-12 leads. To achieve that, we have our own KPI to reach and my goal is to get five sales calls a month by reaching out to prospect leads on social media, reconnecting with past leads, responding to inquiries and contacting potential clients needing Virtual Assistant services.

In addition to my role as Sales Assistant, I also serve as a supervisor for our clients and VAs.

My role involves ensuring both clients and VAs have the support they need to achieve their goals. I support clients in various aspects of their business Whether they need help setting up systems, structuring their operations, or developing strategies. This includes guiding them through the strategies we teach, helping them understand and implement these strategies, and ensuring they have the tools and knowledge to succeed. Additionally, I assist clients with the applications and tools we use, troubleshooting any issues, and providing training to VAs as needed.

On a weekly or monthly basis, I bring significant results to the business, including increased sales through lead generation and sales support, as well as client satisfaction through regular communication and excellent support.

Overall I'm in charge of Sales support, Client and VAs supervisor. This experience taught me the importance of adaptability, continuous learning, and teamwork. It was one of the hardest but also proved to be the most rewarding experiences, allowing me to grow both personally and professionally.

Rei's POV

Hello there, I'm Rei! Working at Empowering Virtual Solution (EVS) as an HR and Recruitment Specialist over the past seven years has been nothing short of transformative. It's a role that has pushed me to grow professionally and personally, adapting to the fast-paced demands of the virtual world.

In the early days, my focus was sharpened on managing our TikTok account, a crucial tool for engaging potential recruits and spreading the word about our services. It started in 2022 as part of the VA Academy Training. As years passed by, we just learned that through consistent sharing of our VAs Client Meet & Greet reels would reach a wider audience that now has 21K Followers and 100K Likes. Each new follower and like was a direct result of the content I created—content that had to be engaging, informative, and aligned with our brand's voice. The thrill of seeing our digital footprint expand was exhilarating, proving that our strategies to captivate an audience were working.

However, managing EVS's TikTok account was just one part of my role. Clear communication was paramount, especially when it came to fostering growth in our *Facebook* group, Empowered Virtual Assistants Network (EVAN), which started in 2020 and immensely grew its members to 23K as of the year 2024. Ensuring that every post, update, and interaction within EVAN was clear and effective helped maintain a vibrant community. This was no small task. It required a meticulous approach to digital communication–every message had to be crafted with the right tone and information to foster trust and encourage engagement from our members.

Adaptability came into play heavily when social media trends shifted or when recruitment strategies needed a revamp. I learned quickly that staying flexible and open to learning new skills was essential. For instance, when recruitment demands spiked, I adapted our strategies to not just meet but exceed our goals. This often meant exploring new platforms or tweaking our messaging to ensure it resonated with a broader audience.

One particular challenge was finding creative solutions to extend our resources without additional costs, such as earning *Airtable* credits to enhance our operational capabilities. I've created the VA Application form using *Airtable* and used the affiliate link to encourage the applicants to sign up to the platform which gave us $10 *Airtable* credits each. It resulted in $36,000 *Airtable* credits or 3,600 signups. Each successful strategy not only saved costs but also improved our efficiency, allowing us to focus more on strategic growth rather than operational limitations.

Gratitude played a subtle yet powerful role in my daily interactions. Recognising the hard work of colleagues and expressing thanks contributed significantly to a positive workplace culture. This appreciation was not just about being polite; it was about building a team that felt valued and motivated.

The journey wasn't always smooth. Earning trust and establishing myself in this role required me to dive deep into the company's culture, actively seek feedback, and consistently deliver results that not only met but exceeded expectations. My initial nerves soon turned into confidence as I took on more responsibilities and contributed to shaping recruitment strategies that have significantly impacted our company's growth.

My tenure at EVS has been a deep dive into the world of virtual assistance, where I have honed my skills in time management, problem-solving, and strategic thinking. The lessons I've learned here—embracing change, the importance of clear communication, and the power of a positive attitude—have shaped me into a more effective leader and a key player in the success of EVS.

In conclusion, my journey at EVS has been about more than just personal and professional growth. It has been about contributing to a team that values innovation and adaptability and using my skills to help scale a business in ways that were once beyond my imagination.

Note to self: Gratitude in Delegation. Show appreciation for those who contribute to your success.

What actions are you going to take from this chapter?

1 _____

_____

_____

_____

_____

2 _____

_____

_____

_____

3 _____

_____

_____

_____

CONCLUSION

∞

Well, we've come a long way together, haven't we? From the first page to this last one, my hope is that you've not just read this book but you've experienced a shift in how you see your role as a leader and the transformative power of delegation.

Remember how it felt to imagine shedding those countless hats, each a burden you were never meant to bear alone? That's not just a dream; it's a feasible reality if you embrace the practices we've explored. Delegation isn't just about freeing up your calendar; it's about freeing your business to reach heights that were impossible when you tried to juggle everything on your own.

As you stand on this side of our journey, equipped with the know-how of hiring, managing, and thriving with Virtual Assistants, think of your business not just as a series of tasks to be completed but as a dynamic entity that grows with each task you delegate. You've learned not just to manage time but to master it, to mould it into a tool that works for you, not against you.

Your Virtual Assistants are more than helpers; they're your partners in this grand adventure of entrepreneurship. As you implement the lessons on effective onboarding, training, and long-term retention, remember that each step forward is a step you don't have to take alone. Your VAs are there, ready to take the reins when you need them to.

And finally, as you close this book and look towards the future, remember why you started your business in the first place. It wasn't to drown in work but to build something great, something that could provide value while allowing you the freedom to enjoy the life you've worked so hard to build. With the power of delegation, you're not just working on your business; you're working towards a better, more fulfilling future.

Thank you for trusting me to guide you through this process. Here's to your success and the many achievements that lie ahead with your ultimate clone–your team of capable, dedicated Virtual Assistants. Remember, the best way to predict the future is to create it, and with delegation, you're doing just that. Let's keep making waves, one delegated task at a time!

AFTERWORD

∞

What a journey this has been! First off, a massive thank you to my incredible team, without whom this book would still be in the realm of 'someday'. You all are the real stars behind the scenes, turning dreams into reality every day.

A special shout out to Natasa and Stuart at the 48 Hour Author book camp. Your guidance was like a lighthouse in the chaotic sea of my thoughts, helping me navigate through the writing and publishing process seamlessly. You've turned what could have been an overwhelming journey into a manageable, even enjoyable one.

I am immensely grateful to every single one of my Virtual Assistants. You are the unsung heroes of this story. Because of your dedication and hard work, I get to work less while accomplishing more—every entrepreneur's dream. Each of you has shown me the power of trust and delegation, transforming not just my business, but also my life.

This book is not just a reflection of my thoughts, but a testament to the collaborative effort of many brilliant minds. To my readers, I hope this book serves as a beacon, guiding you towards unlocking the potential of delegation in your own ventures. Remember, it's not just about working smarter, but about making your work enrich lives – yours and those around you.

And finally, to anyone who's ever felt overwhelmed by the weight of their business, let this be a reminder: you are not alone. There's a whole world of talented individuals ready to share the load and elevate your business to heights you've only imagined. Embrace the power of delegation; it truly can set you free.

Here's to working less and achieving more. To growth, freedom, and beyond–cheers!

ABOUT THE AUTHOR

∞

Francesca landed in Australia in 2009 and started off at a typical 9-5 job. But by 2014, she felt a pull towards something more fulfilling – life coaching – and struck out on her own. Starting a business as a foreigner brought more challenges than she expected, throwing her into the deep end of entrepreneurship.

Despite the crowded market and the steep learning curve, Francesca dived into the habits of successful entrepreneurs, discovering that a blend of online and offline presence was key. Just three months after implementing these strategies, she was fully booked. It was a breakthrough, but Francesca wanted more; she was driven to make a larger impact.

This drive crystallised when several life coaches came to her, eager to learn how she had filled her schedule so quickly. With the opportunity, Francesca launched the Academy to empower other entrepreneurs, business owners, speakers, and coaches to succeed using the strategies she had honed. Over time, she fine-tuned these techniques, teaching her clients to shift from being invisible to invincible, both online and offline.

Her business skyrocketed from earning a modest $120 to pulling in over $1.5 million in less than four years with the help of her Virtual Assistants. She grew a thriving community of over 450 entrepreneurs, creating a supportive network where everyone grows together.

Now, Francesca focuses all her energy on her Virtual Assistant Agency, Empowering Virtual Solution. Here, she continues to make waves globally, connecting time-poor business owners with social media wizards trained in her strategic methods. Remarkably, she skyrocketed this venture to a million-dollar enterprise in just over 14 months.

Francesca Moi is a testament to the power of a visionary mindset in business. Her ongoing dedication to her clients ensures they achieve remarkable successes, proving that anyone can transform their business dreams into reality with the right strategies and a bit of passion.

HIRE A VA

∞

Empower Your Business with Francesca Moi

Ready to kick your business into high gear and finally master that elusive art of delegation and time management? Let's make it happen together! I'm Francesca Moi, and I'm thrilled to introduce you to my Virtual Assistant Agency, *Empowering Virtual Solution*. This isn't just about getting things off your plate; it's about transforming how your business operates.

Imagine having a team of expertly trained Virtual Assistants who handle your day-to-day tasks, freeing you up to focus on big-picture strategies and growth. That's what hundreds of entrepreneurs have achieved working with us, and now it's your turn. Dive into a world where your business runs smoother, grows faster, and feels a whole lot easier to manage.

Join our community of go-getters who've transformed their businesses with a little help from their dedicated virtual teams. It's time to empower your business dreams with real solutions. Let's get started and watch your business soar!

Are you...
- Not having enough time to manage your social media?
- Not having enough time to repurpose your content on *Facebook* and generate more leads?
- Feeling like admin tasks are piling up and taking you away from what you do best?
- Having a hard time with technology and wishing there was someone there that could work it all out for you?

If you've answered YES to one of the questions above, I GET YOU!

We've all been there, working tirelessly for hours and feeling like you are not getting enough done.

Time is never enough, and it's even harder if we don't have anyone cheering us, supporting us, and working it all out for us! You end up feeling stuck and frustrated. You have big dreams and many ideas, and you want to help more and more people, but you don't have the time or energy to scale your business and match your BIG aspirations!

This is the reason why ***Empowering Virtual Solution*** came to life.

This VA program is for time-poor business owners who need a set of helping hands in their business to gain more time and focus more on their zone of genius rather than drowning in doing all things IN their business.

Our team has helped over 100 business owners get their lives back whilst achieving all their business and personal goals. We've trained and supplied over 100 VAs and taught them strategies to achieve the outcome that you want faster and more effectively.

Introduction to Empowering Virtual Solution

Empowering Virtual Solution Ltd Pty is an Australian outsourcing agency that seamlessly connects your business with skilled Virtual Assistants (VAs) from the Philippines. We manage the entire process, including:

- Hiring
- Training
- Project Management
- HR & Payroll
- Disruption/Replacement Cover

Our Unique Approach:
Our support goes beyond matching you with a VA. We provide continuous assistance through an experienced supervisor, help assign tasks to maximise efficiency, and offer access to business coaching and a supportive community of business owners.

Our Process:
To join our team, VAs must:

- Be highly motivated and committed
- Pass a stringent application process
- Complete our specialised training
- Have an approved home workspace

How We Match:
Personality Test: We require a personality test from you to ensure a compatible match.
Skills Assessment: We match VAs based on the specific skills you need.

Your VA is specifically trained in the below Programs:
- Marketing
- Social Media
- Administrative Tasks
- Customer Service Tasks
- Customer Relationship Management

Industries We Serve:

Our VAs are effectively working and driving success in various industries, such as:

- Legal & Immigration
- Real Estate & Construction
- Health & Wellness
- Travel Agencies
- Education & Coaching
- Financial Services & Accounting
- Software & IT
- Marketing & Advertising
- E-Commerce & Retail

Our VAs are integral to the daily operations and growth of businesses across these sectors. They ensure efficiency and allow business owners to focus on strategic initiatives.

OUR PACKAGES:

FULL TIME VA: 40-hour work week
PART TIME VA: 20-hour work week

CONTACT THE TEAM

Get started with your VA Now! Contact us to learn more!

Scan this code:

LEVEL UP CONFERENCE

∞

The Level Up Business Conference is an annual two-day event hosted by Francesca Moi and her team in Brisbane, Australia. This premier conference is dedicated to helping entrepreneurs and business leaders elevate their operations from basic to booming. Each year, we welcome between 80-150 clients and members of the public who join us for a blend of learning, fun, and networking.

Designed for both emerging and established business professionals, the Level Up Business Conference features experienced entrepreneurs, industry experts, and business coaches. They share invaluable insights and experiences, equipping attendees with practical tools for business growth and personal fulfillment.

Key Themes of the Conference:
- Business Software Implementation and Identifying Needs
- Personal Balance and Growth
- Team Development and Leadership
- Event Planning and Networking Opportunities
- And so much more

We also include our clients in a unique way by giving them opportunities to share their experiences on stage, discussing the transformative impact of working with their Virtual Assistants. Additionally, attendees have the chance to win awards, enhancing the community feel of the event.

The Level Up Business Conference is more than just an event; it's a transformative journey. Each session encourages attendees to think bigger, delegate smarter, and lead their businesses to new heights, offering essential tools and insights to navigate challenges and achieve business success

WORK WITH FRANCESCA

1:1 Coaching Sessions with Francesca

Ready to transform your business from the ground up? It's time to dive into my personalised coaching sessions, where we'll tackle everything from crafting razor-sharp business strategies to mastering the art of scalability. Here's what you'll get:

- **Strategic Business Playbooks:** We'll develop actionable strategies that are not just about keeping up but about setting the pace in your industry.
- **Scaling Made Simple:** Learn how to move from the traditional one-on-one business model to a structure that's both profitable and scalable.
- **Social Media & Events Mastery:** I'll show you how to leverage social media and events to significantly elevate your business profile.
- **Mindset Makeover:** Unlock your true potential with a mindset shift that turns obstacles into opportunities.

Why wait to make your business dreams a reality?

Packages:
1 HOUR SESSION - Dip your toes into the world of organic marketing. We'll cover the fundamentals, address your burning questions, and set you on the path to organic success.

2 HOUR SESSION - Ready to dive deeper? In this extended session, we'll not cover only the essentials but also work hands-on to fine-tune your strategies and overcome any roadblocks.

3 HOUR SESSION - For those who crave a comprehensive overhaul, this session is for you. We'll leave no stone unturned as we revamp your organic marketing approach and set you up for long-term growth.

Book a coaching session with me, Francesca, and let's start your journey to business success today! Together, we'll make sure you not only meet your goals but exceed them.

WELCOME TO YOUR MARKETING BREAKTHROUGH

Are you ready to take your brand to the next level?

SCAN THE CODE TO KNOW MORE

Time Management Course

Ever feel like you're running a never-ending race against the clock? I get it, and that's exactly why I've crafted this Time Management Course. It's all about giving you the tools to not just juggle–but truly balance and excel in both your professional and personal life.

Here's what you'll get:

- **Master the Art of Prioritisation:** Learn how to sort your tasks by impact, not just urgency, to really boost your productivity.
- **Practical Time Management Tactics:** I'll show you the strategies that really work to streamline how you handle your daily duties.
- **Find Your Balance:** Because life isn't just about work, discover how to efficiently allocate time to all aspects of your life.
- **Stress Less, Achieve More:** Reach your business goals quicker and with less stress. It's possible, and I'll show you how!

Ready to take control of your time? Enrol in my Time Management Course and start transforming your busy days into your best performance. Let's make every minute count and propel your business to new heights! Enquire now! Please refer to page 215.

Invite Francesca as a Speaker

Looking to electrify your next event with some dynamic insights and strategies? Invite me, Francesca Moi, to speak and I'll bring the energy and expertise that transform an ordinary event into an unforgettable learning experience!

Here's what I'll dive into:

- **Organic Marketing Strategies:** Learn how to supercharge your personal brand without spending a fortune. I'll unpack powerful tactics to enhance visibility and attract your ideal audience organically.
- **Leveraging Virtual Assistants:** Discover how to streamline your operations and supercharge your business growth by integrating skilled Virtual Assistants into your team.
- **Mastering Delegation:** I'll share the secrets to delegating effectively, ensuring every team member plays to their strengths, which boosts productivity and satisfaction.
- **Filling Up Events Organically:** Find out how to fill your events naturally and effectively, creating buzz and excitement without the heavy ad spend.

Don't miss the chance to have me, Francesca Moi, to energise your audience and provide them with actionable insights they can immediately implement to see real results. Let's make your event one that attendees will talk about for years to come!

Take Action Now

Whether you're looking to improve your time management, need one-on-one coaching, or seek a dynamic speaker for your next event, Francesca Moi is the perfect choice to help you and your business thrive.

Contact us today to enrol in the Time Management Course, book a coaching session, or invite Francesca to speak at your event:
Email: info@empoweringvirtualsolution.com
Phone: +61 07 3111 6470
Website: www.empoweringvirtualsolution.com

CAN I ASK A FAVOUR?

Thank you for reading "The Power of Delegation: Save Time, Save Money and Grow with Virtual Assistants." If you found this book helpful, could you please take a moment to leave a review? Your feedback would greatly help get this book into the hands of busy business owners and CEOs who are managing it all solo and might be feeling overwhelmed. Your review could make a significant difference!

Just scan the QR code below to leave your review:

SEND ME YOUR FEEDBACK

SCAN THE CODE TO LEAVE A REVIEW

www.ingramcontent.com/pod-product-compliance
Lightning Source LLC
Chambersburg PA
CBHW031848200326
41597CB00012B/321